Oscar Robertson: The Inspiring Story of One of Basketball's Greatest Point Guards

An Unauthorized Biography

By: Clayton Geoffreys

Table of Contents

Foreword

Oscar Robertson in many ways changed the game of basketball for good. Robertson was the first player in NBA history to average a triple-double for a season, and held this statistic for many years until Russell Westbrook would join him years later. Oscar retired a 12-time All-Star, 11-time All-NBA Team selection and a one-time winner of the Most Valuable Player Award. Thank you for purchasing *Oscar Robertson: The Inspiring Story of One of Basketball's Greatest Point Guards*. In this unauthorized biography, we will learn Oscar Robertson's incredible life story and impact on the game of basketball. Hope you enjoy and if you do, please do not forget to leave a review!

Also, check out my website at claytongeoffreys.com to join my exclusive list where I let you know about my latest books. To thank you for your purchase, you can go to my site to download a free copy of *33 Life Lessons: Success Principles, Career Advice & Habits of Successful People*. In the book, you'll learn from some of the greatest thought leaders of different industries on what it takes to become successful and how to live a great life.

Cheers,

Clayton Geoffreys

Visit me at www.claytongeoffreys.com

Introduction

When looking at some of the best basketball players over the last 30 years, some of the greatest stars tend to be the ones who can basically do it all. They can score, pass, rebound, and do almost anything that can fill the stat sheet up. Of course, numbers tend to be the best measure of the effects of a player on a team because basketball has always been a numbers game.

In that regard, some of the best players that have been able to fill the stat sheet up in a hurry include the likes of LeBron James, Russell Westbrook, Luka Dončić, Scottie Pippen, Grant Hill, Magic Johnson, Nikola Jokić, and several other notable names that have played the sport in the last three to four decades in NBA history. All of those names were great all-around players during their respective prime years.

Due to how the game puts a premium on a player that is capable of doing it all and can fill the stat sheet up, every team in the league wants someone that can play that role to perfection. And every player wants to be able to put up ridiculous stats that are capable of explaining what he can do when he is on the floor and how he affects the game. This is where the triple-double comes into mind as one of the most impressive statistics of all time. A triple-double is when a player collects double digits in three separate statistical categories except for turnovers and fouls. In most cases, triple-doubles involve points, rebounds, and assists, but there have been cases when a player was able to collect a triple-double by recording double digits in either blocks or steals.

When looking at the best triple-double machine in NBA history, one cannot look past what Russell Westbrook has done in his career. He is the only player to have multiple seasons of averaging a triple-double, and he has done it four times when no other player has done it twice. Of course, before

Westbrook, there have been other statistical beasts such as LeBron James, Jason Kidd, and Scottie Pippen, who could all put up triple-doubles from time to time but not at the same rate as Westbrook. But before Westbrook and most of the other great statistical beats in the NBA were even born and before people marveled at how amazing a triple-double is, one of the players that blazed the trail for all of the great all-around stars played at a time when no one in the history of the game has ever seen what he could do. That man is Oscar Robertson.

As a guard playing during the 1960s and the early 70s, Oscar Robertson paved the way for what an all-around player should be like because he could do it all whenever he was on the floor. He could score with the best of them, collect more rebounds than bigger players, and pass the ball like a maestro. This was how he became the first player to average a triple-double in a single season. And for more than five decades, he was the only person who did so, as his record seemed unbeatable until Westbrook shattered it in 2017.

Robertson played during an era that does not have the same refined brand of basketball that we see in today's more modern NBA, making it not too difficult for a transcendent star playing 40 minutes a night to regularly average double digits in rebounds or score 30 or more points. At 6'5", Robertson was bigger than most guards and had the height and build of an old-school forward.

While it might not be surprising for Robertson to have collected a great deal of points and rebounds at that time due to his amazing physical gifts in comparison to his peers, what was more impressive was the fact that he collected double digits in assists during the 60s. Take note that, before Robertson averaged 11.38 assists during the 1961-62 season, no other point guard in history had averaged double digits in assists.

The reason why players struggled to collect assists during this time was the fact that not all players were great at finishing. In the 50s, it was quite normal for players to shoot 30 to 40% from the field, as they did not have the same refined skills that most of today's players. On top of that, the game was quite physical back then, contributing to how difficult it was for some players to finish. But despite these challenges, Oscar Robertson went on to become the first player in NBA history to average double digits in assists. He was a court maestro in every sense of the word because he always had the ball in his hands and knew what to do with it whenever he was in attack mode. The defensive attention that he absorbed allowed his teammates to get good looks that they were able to finish properly.

All that said, the fact that he was bigger than most guards and forwards and that he was as true a playmaker as any playmaker could be allowed Robertson to become the first player to average a triple-double. While triple-doubles were not as hyped-up back then as they are today, it was still an amazing accomplishment for any player to do so during the 60s. And the fact that it took over five decades for someone to do what he did makes it even more impressive.

In a way, Oscar Robertson was a pioneer in terms of what an all-around player could do. Thanks to his all-around prowess as a guard that could do everything all on his own, he was a constant name in the All-Star Game and was always one of the favorites to win the MVP award. However, throughout much of his prime years, Robertson seemed like a one-man show that could not win a championship.

If ever there was something that the Boston Celtics proved during the 60s, it was that a team wins the championship. As great as Bill Russell was, he could not do it all on his own because he had teammates scoring and playmaking for him. Meanwhile, one-man armies like Oscar Robertson and even Wilt Chamberlain struggled to win championships during their prime years. It was during the 1970-71 season when a 32-year old Oscar Robertson left the Cincinnati Royals, a team he played with for ten seasons, to join the Milwaukee Bucks and the 23-year old rising star formerly known as Lew Alcindor and is now known as Kareem Abdul-Jabbar. At that point, he was no longer the all-around threat that he used to be, but was still good enough to put up great stats. But it was by playing with another dominant player and a great team that he was finally able to win his first and only NBA championship.

While Oscar Robertson is not the first name one would think of when it comes to team success in the NBA as, in fairness to him, not a lot of non-Celtics players were able to win titles during the 60s, he is the prototype of the modern-day all-around player that we often get impressed by because of their amazing stats.

Long before Russell Westbrook, LeBron James, or Luka Dončić were putting up dominant all-around numbers, Oscar Robertson was doing it on a nightly basis. And this is what is meant by building on what the greats before were able to establish. While today's all-around stars may have surpassed him, Robertson was one of the true foundations of all-around greatness in the early era of the NBA, as he rightfully deserves being called one of the 75 Greatest Players.

Chapter 1: Childhood and Early Life

Oscar Robertson was born on November 24, 1938, in Charlotte, Tennessee, as the youngest of three children. A small and sickly infant living in a farmhouse, Oscar's mother did not even think that he would survive long enough because he was so frail. His foot also appeared deformed, and so his mother took to massaging it so that he would be able to grow up a normal boy.[i]

At that time, the Robertsons were living in a farming community in Tennessee. The 30s were not exactly the best time for farmers, and one could only think of how bad it was for black farmers at that time. The primary reason why life was so hard for them was the fact that machines were taking over the farming industry in the US, as manual labor was getting replaced by tractors. Unfortunately, the Robertson household did not have the money to buy any of these machines. And on top of that, the nearest school was a white school that did not admit black children. The only opportunity for education that the Robertson kids had was a nearby Mount Zion. Their father realized that the only way for the kids to get a better life was for them to go to a good school.

Bailey Sr., Oscar's father, heard from his aunt that Indianapolis was hiring people of color. At that time, there was no discrimination in defense plants because America needed all the labor it could get during the time of the Second World War. Bailey ventured to Indianapolis to look for a job. However, there were no permanent openings and he had to come home from time to time when he became lonely.

Finally, when the Robertsons were tired of the setup, Oscar's mother Mazell decided to pack up their bags so that they could move in with Bailey Sr. in

Indianapolis. Despite the relocation, the Robertson family still lived a dirt-poor lifestyle that did not offer them a lot of choices and opportunities in life. His family lived in a segregated housing project in Indianapolis throughout much of his entire childhood life.[ii]

The difference between poor kids growing up during the 40s and poor kids living in today's era is quite huge. Back then, Robertson grew up at the time of World War II, which was not the easiest time to live in for any young person. Moreover, during the 40s, racial inequality was still quite prominent, as African-Americans were still segregated. This meant that Oscar Robertson's parents struggled to provide for their children. Bailey Sr. worked in the city sanitation department while earning a humble wage.[iii] However, the Robertson parents made sure that their kids were well-fed. Even though the children knew that they were poor, Oscar never felt that his parents made them know that they were living in poverty because they tried their best to provide for their children. And neither of them talked about race, as it had seemed like they accepted the possibility that they were never going to be given equal rights. Instead, Bailey Sr. mostly preached about how important education was for them because, regardless of how the country was going to treat them, being educated meant that they could bridge the huge gap between them and white people in America.[i]

As a young boy, Oscar learned to play basketball because it was considered a poor person's game at that time. During those days, the most popular sport in the country was baseball, which was quite expensive for anyone poor to play, as it required a bat, as well as a bigger field. What made basketball a poor person's game during those days was that it was something that any person could play anywhere. He mostly played in a run-down and dusty basketball court called the "dust bowl" because it was hardly ever maintained on the side of town that was reserved and segregated for the African-American community. It was simply a makeshift court that some person put up when he realized that the lot was vacant.

But the Robertsons were too poor to afford a real basketball. That was when Oscar first truly felt the sting of poverty. This was when he resorted to using just about anything just so he could play basketball during his free time. He used old tennis balls to shoot through the basket. And when he was at home, he rolled up some old rags into a ball and shot them on a wall while pretending that he was shooting through a real hoop.

Life was indeed tough for Oscar Robertson as a child. But he had the imagination and creativity that allowed him to make the most out of his situation. As he grew older, his parents were able to earn enough to provide for his needs as a growing athlete. That was also when he realized that his brother, Bailey Jr., was one talented player because of his ability to shoot the ball. Growing up looking up to older brothers allowed Oscar to have role models in the sport.

One of the best things about Oscar's humble beginnings was the fact that he was much more focused on playing sports than anything else. He was primarily a basketball player, but he still learned how to play baseball. Oscar and his brothers were outdoor kids that played any kind of sport they could play during their free time. And he rarely watched television or listened to the radio, except when there was a black boxer fighting because that was a moment of pride for the African-American community in the country.[i]

Family life was also a central part of the Robertson household while Oscar was growing up. It was not rare for him and his extended family members to meet up whenever they could, despite the fact that his parents were

8

struggling with their own relationship. Eventually, Bailey Sr. and Mazell divorced when Oscar was 11, but he did not find out about it until he reached high school because they still lived in the same house. Bailey Sr. valued raising his children over moving out. Of course, it was also expensive for any of the two parents to move out of the house.

It was also right around the age of 11 when Oscar Robertson received his first true basketball. This was not a brand-new ball because it was about to be thrown away by the family that his mother was working for as a maid.[iii] She took the opportunity to ask for it from that family so that she could give it as a present to her son. And that was one of the core events in the young Oscar's life because owning a basketball allowed him to play the sport to his heart's content.

When Robertson reached his middle school years, he enrolled at Crispus Attucks, an all-black school that was run by a black principal and black professors that had doctorate degrees. They were not allowed to work or teach at an all-white school due to segregation. And at the time Oscar went to school there, his brother Bailey Jr. was already a sophomore playing for the Attucks high school basketball team.

A good part of Oscar's middle school years was spent watching his brother play. Bailey, nicknamed Flap, was a third-string 5'9" guard that hardly got the opportunity to play. As a sophomore, he was even left off the team for reasons that the coach never revealed. But during the 1951 regional finals, one of the most memorable and inspiring moments of Oscar Robertson's life happened when he watched his brother help the Attucks Tigers win against the Anderson Indians, an all-white school, even though he was only there as a substitute for the team's starting guard, who had fouled out.

Flap wanted to prove to his coach that he could play if he was just given a chance to do so. That was when he helped his team come back from a ten-point deficit by scoring four of the team's points. Of course, he was the one who drained the game-winning jumper when all of his teammates were double-teamed by the opposing team. The entire community was elated by what Flap did because victories in sports were the only victories the black people could have over their white counterparts at that time. And sports was always something that got black communities together because they knew that, even if they were not allowed to excel in the other facets of society, they could still work hard to become great athletes.

"People told me their relatives died of heart attacks," Flap said. "One lady said when the ball went through the hoop, she started going into labor."[i]

The victory did not seem much in the greater scheme of things. But Flap's performance in that game inspired an entire community. Of course, it also inspired Oscar Robertson to believe that if his brother could do something like that, he could also achieve something just as big or even bigger. It was that moment that made Oscar believe that basketball was going to be a huge part of his life. Flap's shot sparked hope and joy in his heart because, according to him, everything changed in that game. Robertson's world would never be the same again after that game-winning shot from his brother.

After Flap's shot, Robertson started spending more time on the court. This time, he no longer had to spend more time on the old dust bowl because a new asphalt court was erected in Indianapolis's first public housing project called Lockefield Gardens. After school, Oscar practically lived on the Lockefield courts. He did his chores promptly and always made sure he finished his schoolwork before he made his way to the courts. So, if he was not at home doing his chores or at school during a school day, he could be found playing basketball with his secondhand ball.

The shot that Flap made inspired an entire generation of black players living in the black community around Indianapolis. After that shot, Oscar noticed that the Lockefield courts were always full of different players. Adults played alongside and against high school and middle school players on the court, as the victory that the Attucks Tigers had over the Anderson Indians made everyone believe that they too could have a victory over life as big as what the local high school team had accomplished. However, Oscar Robertson was too young to be running with the older and better players on the court. He needed to earn his keep by going to the courts early so that the teams playing on the court would choose him because they had no choice. Coming over to the court late would mean that there would be players chosen ahead of him, and that meant that his chances of playing against the older, bigger, and better players were slim. And Oscar took every opportunity he had whenever he had a chance to play with the best local players. But there was also a pecking order that Oscar and his friends needed to respect. Due to the lack of available courts, they needed to prove their worth because the older and stronger players would not allow them to play. That was why he needed to prove himself every chance he had because not a lot of young players were given opportunities to play by the more dominant personalities in the neighborhood. And Oscar initially struggled to prove himself.

The bigger and older were always going to post him up, push him around the court, or even jump over him whenever they had the chance to do so. Oscar needed to learn how to deal with being bullied by other players on the court because he knew that the only way he could prove himself was to absorb everything they had to throw at him. Things such as learning how to hold his ground whenever he was being pushed around or knowing how to escape double teams in the backcourt were things that he needed to go through back then. But while he did struggle at the beginning, everyone around him noticed that he was improving.

Robertson saw the beatings and the tough experiences he had as learning opportunities he needed to go through so that he would become better. He ran the gauntlet and came out of it with skills that no one else had. On top of that, his understanding of the game improved as he grew in experience playing against some of the toughest competitors in the neighborhood. The tough situations the older players were making him go through also improved the way he handled the game. During his early teen years, he was already good enough to see the court and to understand how plays were going to develop because of the double teams and the different defenses that the older players were throwing at him. By the time he reached a certain level of skill and understanding, he was receiving praise from older teenagers and adults alike.

He went on to say that so much of what he learned as a fundamentally sound basketball player was due to his playground experiences during his younger years. He did play in high school and college, but he did not learn much about basketball during his formal playing years. Instead, it was the informal and unstructured style of basketball in the playground that allowed him to develop more as a player.[i]

Robertson's middle school coach started calling him Li'l Flap because he was the brother of Flap Robertson, one of the rising stars in the Attucks high school team. However, Oscar believed that he and Flap were very different from one another precisely because his brother hardly ever played with him.

Bailey Jr. was a flash and aggressive player that loved to talk whenever he was on the court. He was more outgoing than his younger brother and had a game that was full of style and personality. On the other hand, Oscar was more of a fundamentally sound player that let his game do the talking. He did not have the flashiest game, but he could still beat bigger and older players with his fundamental skills and advanced understanding of the sport. And he was also very polite to his teammates and opponents alike.

Nevertheless, during his seventh grade, Oscar eventually learned what it meant to play organized basketball, which was different from the game he was used to on the Lockefield courts. His skills were more in line with what could be seen on the playground, and that meant that he needed to be coached the right way. Tom Sleet, his middle school coach, drilled the basics of dribbling, passing, and pivoting to him. And the fact that he was learning more about the game got Oscar excited to go to practice every day.

But the problem back then was that the only fundamentals that the players were taught at a young age were three things: passing, catching, and pivoting. That is because the basic idea of the sport of basketball was pretty simple back then. A player should pass the ball to an open player, who would catch the ball and pivot to look for the next open player. Motion offense was at its simplest form because players needed to pass, catch, and pivot until they found the player who had the highest chance to score against their defender. In that regard, almost every young player was playing that style back then. It was difficult for other players to have a sense of identity because they were taught the same things, regardless of what positions they played. From a fundamental standpoint, there is nothing wrong with that. However, from the standpoint of an individual player, the only way to stand out was to be better at passing, catching, and pivoting or to be taller and bigger than anyone else.

That was why the center position was the most important role for any player back then because they were always in the better position to score due to how the game was played.

Oscar Robertson, however, wanted to maintain a sense of identity. That was why, after school practices, he stayed in the practice facility or went over to the playground to focus on things that the coaches had not been teaching him. He practiced his layups, tip-ins, and crossovers. He also mastered the art of dribbling with his left hand. The best thing was that his coach encouraged him because Oscar simply just loved playing the game, regardless of whether or not he was going to eventually become a professional. And he was thankful for having such a supportive coach guiding him.

Chapter 2: High School Career

Robertson continued to work under Tom Sleet, who also coached the Crispus Attucks freshman team. Meanwhile, it was Ray Crowe who worked on coaching the varsity team, as Robertson saw the early effects of what it meant to play a non-aggressive style of basketball. At that time, because black high school teams wanted to minimize the chances of escalating their relationship with white high school teams, the focus of most coaches was to teach their kids to learn how to play a style that minimized the need to be aggressive and physical. Black players were taught to keep a good distance away from other players when playing defense. And whenever they were passing and shooting, they needed to keep their feet on the ground. This was what Oscar believed became the downfall of Attucks whenever they played against white teams. They were not allowed to play an aggressive and physical brand of basketball, despite the fact that their opponents were playing physically. And Crowe was also a bit vocal about not liking Flap Robertson's personality because he played the same way, which would have made him a good player in today's modern era.

The fact that Flap was someone who could start a fight and even a riot with his brash style of basketball was what kept him out of the championship game that the Tigers played after he drained that game-winning shot in the regional finals. They eventually lost in the state finals to a team that was used to physical play because that team's starters also played for the school's football team.[i]

As good as Bailey Jr. was in high school, he couldn't get a college scholarship from one of the bigger programs in Indiana. He went on to become a star at Indiana Central College, a small program. Flap was able to lead the team well enough to the top of the national rankings for small colleges, all while he was consistently scoring in bunches. However, due to the fact that he did not have a real shot at the pros, he settled for a career with the Harlem Globetrotters after becoming one of the greatest players Indiana Central College had ever seen.

Meanwhile, Oscar Robertson was ready to carve out his own career at Crispus Attucks high school. At the end of his freshman year, he was already a little over 5'8" and was quite lanky. But it was a good thing that puberty kicked in for him at the right time and in the right place when he was spending most of his summer at the farm back in his hometown in Tennessee.

Every summer, Oscar and his family went back home so that they could spend their time there. On the farm, he was more than willing to put in the necessary work to help out in any way he could. Putting in the work on the fields allowed him to stay in shape the entire time. And all this work allowed his muscles to grow as he grew taller during his growth spurt.

By the time Oscar Roberts entered his sophomore year in high school, he was almost 6'3", a pretty good size for any guard at that time. On top of that, he also became more muscular. He was no longer the lanky kid that struggled to play against the bigger and stronger players over at Lockefield. Instead, he looked like a young boy in the body of a grown man.

As a sophomore in high school during the 50s, a kid that measured nearly 6'3," though an undersized player today, was already big enough to play one of the forward positions'. However, Oscar's size already allowed him to play down low where he could get easier baskets over smaller players. And when his other skills, such as his ability to bring the ball and his coordination were factored in, he became an instant matchup nightmare for any post player willing to guard him.

During his varsity tryouts as a sophomore, Robertson had a choice to make between playing for the varsity team or the junior varsity team during scrimmages. However, one of his friends on the varsity team called him and told him to play for them. And he found out later on that Coach Crowe told his players to try to work Oscar over so that they could see what he could do with the varsity team.

While Robertson could have dominated if he had opted to play for the junior varsity team during that tryout game, he turned out to be better off playing for the varsity team. That was because Crowe loved the fact that he did not try to do too much by dominating the ball and going for a basket every time he could. Instead, he played within the flow of the game': something a coach loved to see from any player, as they needed to focus on what was happening in the game so that they could focus on doing what they were supposed to do.

Ray Crowe loved Robertson's leadership skills and the way he handled himself out on the floor together with the older varsity members. It was as if he knew something about the sport that the other players did not know, and that was what made him special. Even when he was matched up against the regular starters while playing for the second-stringers of the varsity team, he still found a way to affect the game. Of course, Robertson was already used to playing against some of those other guys in the playground, and his competitive juices boiled when he saw them on the other end of the court.

Robertson made the cut, and that was what allowed him to grow from Bailey Jr.'s little brother into his own person. From a more reserved young man, he started opening himself to other people after his confidence improved. 'He said that going to an all-black school allowed him to find his own identity because he felt at home with the other people in the community, and that was not something he would have experienced had he gone to an integrated school where the white kids might make him feel inferior.[i] However, in Attucks, his confidence grew because he felt at home. On top of that, he was also one of the team's best players. Still, Robertson needed to make another adjustment as a player. Spending nearly his entire life as a perimeter player that loved to take the ball to the basket off the dribble, Robertson was asked to play forward because the team's tallest player was just about half an inch taller. They needed their tallest players to rebound and score at the post, and Oscar was their second-tallest player at that time. In hindsight, that was probably the reason why he eventually became the NBA's best rebounding guard.

But while the Attucks Tigers were supposed to have a down season that year, they actually played well, even with Robertson playing forward. Still, one thing led to another, especially when racial issues between black and white teams were still very apparent during that era. The problem was that the Tigers were going to face their rival squad Arsenal Tech, a team primarily composed of white kids. The problem arose when there was an allegation about black teenagers threatening the life of one of the Arsenal Tech starters several days before the game. Tensions continued to escalate from there because several other players were receiving threats. Robertson's life was also threatened by an unknown caller, who told him his life would be in danger if he played against Arsenal Tech.[ii]

A total of five teenagers received death threats in that heated game between Crispus Attucks and Arsenal Tech. Such was the situation decades ago when racial tensions were really serious. Police and FBI agents were stationed in the gym, as there were more than 10,000 people in the building—a new record for a high school regular-season game in Indiana. Of course, the crowd was composed of both black and white fans who were all aware of the growing tensions between the two teams.

Oscar Robertson finished that game with 14 points to help his team win a sloppy and low-scoring bout. He was one of the game-changers in that tense game against their rivals. But according to him, he was not the best sophomore player because that season was full of peaks and valleys for him. There were moments where he scored exceptionally well and played well enough to help his team win. However, there were also instances where he felt quite sloppy. And that was normal for a growing and learning teenager. Then again, even though Robertson could have outrun or outjumped all of the other players at that point in his career, the Tigers focused on playing a smart and systematic game of basketball. Learning the basics, such as passing the ball around at least three times before finding the best shot opportunity was good for his development. And Attucks played a smart style of basketball that focused on teamplay instead of putting the ball in the hands of the best player—a play that is often seen in high school teams today.

Because he focused on creating for others and allowing his teammates to also affect the game in their own way, Robertson was not really a standout sophomore when it came to his stats. But everyone knew that he was gifted and was going to have one of the greatest high school careers in Indianapolis because he did not play like a sophomore.

However, the biggest move that Ray Crowe made ultimately affected Robertson's entire style of play. The Attucks Tigers suffered several injuries, which led to a loss in a rematch against their rivals. That meant that Crowe needed to adjust his lineup because they were missing several different key players that were filling in important spots for the team. Therefore, Crowe, out of convenience and not because he wanted to try to create the world's first big point guard, gave Oscar Robertson the role of the primary ball-handler. He was their *de facto* point guard at the backcourt, and that ultimately led to Oscar developing as a ball-handler in the long run, even though he had the size of a forward.

Robertson always had ball-handling skills for a kid that stood taller than all of the other guards in the high school ranks. As a 6'3" sophomore, he was never boxed into a specific role because many of the things he learned about basketball were due to his efforts in the local playgrounds, causing him to develop ball-handling skills that were quite rare for a kid standing 6'3". And Ray Crowe knew that one of his brightest young players was a capable leader and playmaker whenever the ball was in his hands.

Despite the fact that Robertson was the team's *de facto* point guard on a squad that was undersized but was full of great athletes, he still continued to do all of the things that forwards were expected to do. On offense, he ran the plays and made things easier for his teammates. Meanwhile, on defense, Robertson still hustled for the rebounds and did his best to defend the basket. This was the early makings of arguably the greatest all-around player in the history of the game of basketball.

The fact that the team needed to play a running game due to being undersized meant that they also needed to improve their conditioning. Crowe ran the practices longer and forced the basics of pressing defense and an aggressive and fast style of offense into his players. They did not have size on their side, but that would not matter if they could pressure backcourt players on defense and outrun everyone on offense.

Attucks' new strategy worked to their advantage because Robertson became an instant matchup nightmare for smaller guards but could score inside with the forwards and centers thanks to his size. This came in handy when he consistently drove to the basket to get fouls in the semifinals win over Columbus during his sophomore season in high school. However, the Tigers lost their next game as they failed to win a title that season.

During the summer of his junior year, Robertson finally accepted the fact that his parents were divorced. His dad re-married and had to move to another home after spending nearly four years with his family, even though both he and Mazell were divorced. This forced the Robertson family to move out because Mazell could not make the payments. But growing up in a devoutly religious family made it difficult for Oscar to understand the concept of divorce. This was not something he knew a lot about, as he was forced to come to terms with the fact that he would not have his father around in their new home anymore.

Robertson described his new home as an improvement because it was bigger and just as nice as any home that a struggling black family could afford. His mother still had to work two full-time jobs, despite the fact that Bailey Jr. was already in a full ride in college. But Oscar was appreciative of the fact that his mother never forgot about taking care of them no matter how tired she was.[i]

Meanwhile, Oscar also did his part during that summer. Instead of working for his family's farm back in Tennessee, he got a job paving asphalt for a construction crew. It did not pay a lot but what was important was that he was contributing to the family's expenses. He also built a hoop in his dad's new home, which was only a few blocks away, so that he could spend time working on his game whenever he had some free time. And thanks to the work he put himself through as a manual laborer during the summer, he kept himself in good shape.

Of course, he still played pickup basketball whenever he had the chance to do so. By that time, the entire neighborhood and even the other localities in Indianapolis already knew who he was. People were fighting over the opportunity to play with Oscar because the unwritten rules stated that the winning team gets to stay on the court. And having a high school standout on their team meant that they had a better chance of staying on the court.

His summer days prior to his junior year also contributed to the reason why Robertson never liked dunking the basketball during his entire basketball career. He could dunk because he was always a terrific athlete that also competed in high and long jumps in track and field events. But the problem was that the courts he played in the neighborhood did not have a lot of space between the backboard and the pole.

At one point, he dunked the ball, but he was fouled hard. Since then, he did not try dunking the ball in any regulation game because he felt that doing so was going to be dangerous for someone who always gets fouled by opposing defenses. A hard foul from the defense may end up becoming a career-ending injury for Robertson.

The fact that he did not dunk the ball also allowed him to master the fundamentals of laying the ball into the basket. Today's athletes, whenever they have the chance, try to dunk the ball hard on any person protecting the basket because they can simply outjump them. But Robertson mastered the art of putting his body between the ball and the defender whenever he went up for a shot near the basket. That way, he did not have to jump too high to the point that a landing could mean a possible injury. At the same time, it allowed him to score points effectively against bigger players protecting the basket.

Working through the summer allowed Oscar Robertson to build up the hype surrounding him and his team. He was already labeled the best high school player in the entire city. Meanwhile, the Crispus Attucks Tigers were also regarded as the clear favorites that season. And they might have also been the favorites to win the state championship: something that had not been done by an Indianapolis team in the entire history of the state tournament.

Coach Ray Crowe also allowed the entire team to run a free offense that was no longer hampered by a systematic way of passing the ball around to get open shots. Instead, the Tigers ran the floor hard enough, especially with a guard standing more than 6'3", carrying the ball up the court. Oscar Robertson had become a clear star that the entire city wanted to see play. And because of his amazing play on the floor, the Attucks Tigers only lost one regular-season game during the 1954-55 season.

Heading into the playoffs, the Tigers were 21-1. Robertson was branded the best player of the tournament by the local newspapers, even though one of his teammates shot 70% from the floor and grabbed 21 rebounds per night.[i] That was because Oscar was the one dictating the offense for the team to make every shot easy for the rest of his teammates.

The Tigers dominated their way through the early part of the state tournament. While Crispus Attucks had to claw their way through a victory against their semifinals opponents, a timely interception made by Robertson gave them the ticket that they needed to get to ultimately get to the state finals, where they ended up making history for the entire city of Indianapolis by becoming the first all-black team to make it there.

Crispus Attucks ended up facing Roosevelt in the finals, as Robertson realized that the team was already too tired after barely surviving their previous game. Meanwhile, the Tigers were simply too big, too fast, and too hungry for them in what was a surprising game for many Indianapolis fans because there were no white players on either team.

However, as the Attucks team continued to dominate the opposing team, Robertson realized that the crowd's cheers were getting louder and louder, as both black fans and white fans cheered for what was one of the greatest teams ever assembled in Indiana high school history. As the Tigers passed the century mark, it was all but done because they were simply too good.

Robertson's Attucks team made history by winning the state championship for their school and by becoming the first high school team in Indianapolis history to win the title. Of course, throughout the final three games of the tournament, Robertson scored a total of 97 points, which broke the previous record for the most points scored by a player in a three-game stretch in the state tournament. He scored 30 points in the state championship game, as Oscar Robertson not only solidified himself as a champion, but also as the best player in Indianapolis high school at that time. But the problem was that Oscar Robertson eventually felt how hard it was to be a successful black man because no one would ever celebrate the success of a team that had just won the biggest game of their entire lives. They were not even allowed to enjoy the same kind of motorcade that the other previous schools were allowed to enjoy. And that was because Robertson believed that the mayor was afraid of black people possibly causing a ruckus.

The Attucks Tigers were escorted by the police and were brought back to their all-black neighborhood without the luxury of the same treatment that the other teams in the past were able to receive. Oscar did not even stay at the team's bonfire too long because he immediately caught a ride to his father's house when he saw the opportunity to do so. And when his father asked about his problem, he merely said, "They don't want us."[i]

Regardless, Robertson still felt some of the luxuries that being a state champ offered. The team was given a chance to dine at a good restaurant in downtown Indianapolis. There were also several civic groups that invited him and the team over to different events to celebrate their championship victory. However, in the back of his mind, Oscar felt that being able to go to downtown Indianapolis for any kind of occasion, regardless of whether he was a champion or not, should be something that any black man should be able to enjoy. He tasted what the normal life of a white man was in Indiana but, for him and his teammates, that life was something they could only enjoy after fighting for a championship throughout a long season. These were luxuries that any man in the city should have been able to enjoy. But for him and his teammates, only a state championship was good enough for the city to accept them.

Nevertheless, Robertson did not rest on his laurels. Throughout the offseason and the summer, he spent time playing basketball in the local courts because he needed to make sure that he was still at the top of his game and that he and his teammates would once again reign supreme over the entire state the next season. And because he was the only senior returning to the team the next season, he needed to take on a bigger leadership role for the Tigers. Of course, the Attucks team was so unstoppable that Oscar Robertson and his teammates breezed through the entire regular season. They went undefeated and extended their winning streak to 45 straight games all the way from the previous season. And the most impressive thing about that feat was the fact that Indiana was a hotpot for basketball talent and that every high school team had a star that was good enough to earn a scholarship for a major college program.

Crispus Attucks took their regular-season undefeated streak to the playoffs and did not lose a single game. Robertson remembered that they had an average winning margin of at least 20 points throughout the entire state tournament because he and his teammates were simply too good for the other programs. Robertson was named Indiana's Mr. Basketball, as it was official that no other high school player in the state was better than him after he had just won his second straight state championship. After winning the title, he noticed that they still took the same route that their motorcade in 1955 had taken. The treatment was no different, and that meant that the mayor and the rest of the city still feared a possible riot from the black people in the city. Nevertheless, Robertson had grown to become indifferent to how the team was treated. That was because there was something bigger brewing for Indianapolis, as he was ready to leave the program to go to college.

Schools around the city were starting to accept black kids into their institutions, as school integration was becoming increasingly common back then. Robertson believed that the city was afraid of how unstoppable Crispus Attucks was becoming because all of the best black athletes were concentrated in one single school. For the sake of parity and in the hopes of finding the next Oscar Robertson, more and more schools were beginning to accept black kids. And while the schools' motives were for the sake of sports, Robertson was still proud of the fact that he was able to lead the charge in racial integration in schools in Indiana.

After dominating the state championship, he took part in an All-Star game between the best players of Indiana and Kentucky, as both of these states claimed the sport of basketball as their own. Robertson matched up against

Kentucky's best player, Kelly Coleman, who he completely dominated in that blowout win, to which Coleman made an excuse about his bad leg.

After the game, the coach of the Kentucky team was all praises for Oscar Robertson, who he described as a "pro playing against a bunch of high school players." He also went on to say that Robertson was the best high school player he had ever seen in his life. Praises such as those might have even solidified his claim as the greatest high school player in the entire nation. After all, out of the 108 voters who voted for the Star of Stars in high school in 1956, 106 voted for Robertson.[i]

Robertson finished his high school career with more than 70 colleges all over the country recruiting him. Only Wilt Chamberlain, who graduated from high school a year ago, earned more attention than he did. Of course, he and Chamberlain would go on to become two of the most statistically ridiculous players in the history of the sport of basketball.

Colleges were already recruiting Robertson as early as his sophomore year. However, he held out on accepting offers until his senior year when things started getting out of hand in terms of the calls he was receiving from different programs all over the country. Robertson later mentioned that he did not really enjoy the entire recruitment process because he was more cautious about it. The reason why he was so cautious was that he was about to enter a world that he did not know. For him, the world of traveling on a plane to visit different colleges around the country and receiving complementary money from the recruiters was something that black people were not used to. And there were also instances where black players were not particularly welcome in colleges dominated by white players.

In a way, Robertson was afraid of the recruitment process, but not too afraid to the point that he was not ready to face it. Instead of rushing into the unknown, he spent time calculating and planning for the future because the place he would decide to go to college was going to affect his chances as a professional basketball player. Bailey Jr., for instance,' having played for a smaller school, was not able to find a good college and did not have a chance to go to the NBA no matter how well he played.

The good thing about the NCAA eligibility rules at that time was that colleges were not allowed to talk to players and actively recruit them before high school was already over. This meant that Robertson had enough time to think about where he wanted to go to college without having to worry about different schools selling their programs to him before he could even give himself a minute to think. Of course, he increased his chances of avoiding contact by sports recruiters. After basketball season was over, he focused on the track team and qualified for the state championships in the high jump. Considering that he was still involved with high school sports, he could not be contacted by any college recruiter. This gave him more time to contemplate his future in college.

Growing up in Indiana, one of the dreams that Robertson, as well as every Indiana player had, was playing for Indiana University. They wanted the mystique that came with being a Hoosier. But he had reservations about Indiana coach Branch McCracken, who was said to have a distrust for black players. Several years ago, he recruited Hallie Bryant, who was the best player on Crispus Attucks during Flap's time with the team. But McCracken did not give him enough playing time in college, and this meant that Bryant's potential was wasted there. There was also the fact that he did not even try to recruit Flap at all, despite Bailey Jr.'s tremendous talent.

A year ago, Wilt Chamberlain also rejected Indiana's offer because he thought that McCracken was not too fond of black players, regardless of how talented they were. Indiana was one of the four schools that Chamberlain wanted to attend, but he ultimately chose to go to Kansas and became the world's best college player.

Ray Crowe drove Oscar Robertson to Indiana University for a meeting with McCracken. However, there was no warm visit from the head coach. The secretary told Robertson that McCracken was busy, and that forced the young man to wait for about 30 minutes before the Indiana coach was ready to receive him. And when he was finally able to talk to McCracken face to face, the coach told him that he hoped that Oscar was not the kind of player that wanted to play for money. Insulted, Robertson left without saying a word. Money was never something that Robertson was taught to covet above everything else in the world. His parents taught him well enough to work hard in whatever he did in life, regardless of whether he was going to make a lot of money out of it. He might have been poor, but he was not poor enough to want to play for a coach who thought that all he wanted to be in life was someone who made a lot of money. Robertson said that had McCracken told him right then and there that he wanted the young man to play for his team, he would have signed up for them at that very moment. But getting insulted immediately turned Robertson off.[i] He crossed out the school that he originally wanted to go to because the head coach himself thought so little of his personal values in life.

Meanwhile, the legendary John Wooden of UCLA wanted Oscar Robertson to join him and even sent him his Pyramids of Success to convince the young man to sign up. However, in 1956, Wooden was yet to become the greatest college head coach. And Robertson thought that Los Angeles was too far away for him to be able to go home when he needed to do so.

Robertson also tried his hand at Michigan State because he thought that Michigan was close enough for a long bus ride home. He boarded a plane for the very first time, seemingly more nervous about hopping on an aircraft than meeting the head coach. However, after waiting at the airport for a long time, the coach told him that they had forgotten that he was coming for a visit. He hopped on a plane ride back home on the next flight.

Then there was Walter Paul, who worked as a recruiter for the University of Cincinnati, who heard about Robertson from Crispus Attucks fans in Cincinnati. That was when he tried his hand at recruiting Robertson by actually getting to know more about the young man, who he had never heard of before. Paul spoke with Crow and Oscar's parents to try to convince him to sign up for Cincinnati. Eventually, after learning more about Robertson, Paul was able to set up a meeting that included Oscar and Cincinnati head coach George Smith. Paul was so obsessed with getting the young man to sign up with Cincinnati that his father had become angry with him for neglecting family business so that he could chase after a basketball player. That was how much he wanted Oscar Robertson to play for his team.

Paul and Smith talked Robertson through the program over at Cincinnati, as their students were allowed to divide 28 weeks into 14 weeks for school and 14 weeks for working. Robertson was promised that he was going to be paid a regular wage scale on his job while attending university. On top of that, he also met a lawyer named Jake Brown, who was kind to him and promised him that he would see Oscar's career through right after college so that he could not only end up with a good professional career but would also be able to do well in business with the money that he was making.

Even though Cincinnati had the same demographics as Indiana in the sense that black people were not all that welcome and that the school itself had an all-white team and coaching staff, Robertson thought that the people he had just met were quite sincere and kind to him. Being black did not matter to him anymore at that very moment because he was talking to white people who were kind and sincere enough with their approach.

On June 8, 1956, Robertson graduated from his high school, ranked 16th out of 170 students. The day after he graduated, he announced publicly that he was going to be attending the University of Cincinnati, which was just two hours away from Indianapolis.

Robertson got what he wanted. He was going to a school close to his home and was going to receive a good education from a respectable university. On top of that, he had a chance to play basketball for a program that respected him regardless of the color of his skin. Robertson, through his innate talents and hard work, was going to college and was well on his way to a promising career in basketball—something that not all black teenagers could dream of back in the 1950s.

Chapter 3: College Career

Back in Oscar Robertson's time, college was an important part of a basketball player's career because playing against college competition allowed the players to develop some of the fundamental aspects of their skills while also adjusting to an entirely different competitive environment. It was rare not only during the 50s and 60s but also in the 70s and 80s for players to skip college so that they could go straight to the NBA. However, during the 90s and early 2000s, it became a norm when Kobe Bryant, Tracy McGrady, LeBron James, and Dwight Howard skipped college to go to the NBA and became stars in the professional league. Nowadays, one-and-done college players are essentially in the same boat because they only go to college as a requirement by the NBA and not because they actually wanted to go to college for one year. Then again, it is understandable why players skip the college experience or simply stay there for one year. After all, they are sacrificing four years of possibly making millions of dollars in the NBA if they decide to finish the entire four-year college eligibility. Robertson admitted that if he had the same luxury back then, he would have probably done the same thing.[i] But in 'his time, the college experience was an indispensable part of an athlete's growth. Professional basketball players in the NBA are demanded to be mature enough to know what to do whenever they are out there on the court. And with such a smaller market back in Robertson's time, teams could not afford to make a mistake in the draft because they needed someone mature enough and developed well enough in the collegiate ranks to contribute to the NBA right away.

Of course, college teams were also careful in how they handled their players. Back then, they had freshmen teams that were designed to allow their first-year players to adjust to college life first before they were allowed to play on the main team. The idea was that players were going to play until their third or fourth years in college, and that is why the freshmen team was designed to allow these players to develop steadily at their own pace.

That one year of adjustment was no less important for Robertson. It was the first time in his life that he was living away from his family. He initially did not like the environment in Cincinnati because he did not know anyone. On top of that, he thought that he lived in a particularly warmer part of town and that his room was worse than what he originally thought it would be. On top of that, the people at the University of Cincinnati were not all the same as him because the school only allowed the cream of the crop to enroll. He was now attending school with a majority of white people because at the time, only the white population had the luxury of earning the right to go to a top college.

While Robertson was promised by George Smith that he would not experience racial issues in the school, there were things that basketball coaches could not control. He felt that he did not belong during his freshman year because students would instantly wear shocked faces whenever they saw him walking into classrooms. This was a different experience for him, as back at Crispus Attucks, he felt at home because the people who were similar to him. But Cincinnati did not feel anything close to home.

The classes were especially rough on Robertson, with professors that were allegedly making life difficult for him. But despite the fact that he was told that black people did not go to the University of Cincinnati, he hung on and decided to stay. He could have transferred to another school, but Robertson stuck with the course and let his schoolwork and performance on the court do the talking. And while he initially was not fond of Cincinnati, he eventually ended up spending a good part of his life in that city.

Robertson eventually opened his freshman basketball season against the varsity team, which had improved tremendously under George Smith the last few years. In that game, the varsity team won, but Robertson showed why he was worth every effort. He had 37 points, 17 rebounds, and 8 assists in that game and ended up averaging 33 points per game during his freshman year, as his team went 13-2. And most importantly, thanks to Roberson's brilliance, fans of the team were actually looking to watch the freshmen team more than they did the varsity team'.

Eventually, Oscar Robertson was elevated to the varsity squad during his sophomore year in college, and rightfully so because he was way too dominant on the freshmen team. On the varsity squad, he played several levels above everyone else, and so it did not take too long for him to assert himself as the team's best player. Robertson did not remember a great deal from his first game in varsity, but having scored28 points and finished with 14 assists, what he did know was that it was the first time he was referred to by Dick Baker, the Cincinnati Bearcats' play-by-play announcer, as "The Big O," a nickname that stuck with him throughout his entire career.[i]

As the season went on, The Big O continued to score 30 or more points every single game. He led the entire nation in scoring during the early part of the season. Then, after ten games, he averaged at around 30 points while the team was dominant in the conference. Robertson was so much of a one-man machine that people began calling the Cincinnati Bearcats the "Firehouse Fo and the Big O."

Then came his first-ever game at Madison Square Garden in his first-ever trip to New York City, where the Bearcats were invited to play in a small tournament so that people all over the country could watch Robertson and what he could do. At that point, he was one of the most dominant players in

34

college, averaging 30 points and 16 rebounds. Had Wilt Chamberlain not been playing for Kansas as a junior that season, Robertson might have been the best college player in the entire nation.

In his first game in New York, Robertson used the excitement of playing in the Mecca of basketball as his fuel. He just kept scoring and scoring while also outrunning and outgunning Seton Hall, their opponents, throughout the entire game. The moment he was pulled out of the game with under three minutes left, Seton Hall scored 54 points. Meanwhile, Robertson had 56 points—two more points than what the entire opposing team scored that game.

Robertson's performance allowed him to set a single-game Cincinnati record. On top of that, he also set a record for most points scored by a player in Madison Square Garden. Nobody in the NBA at that time scored more points than Robertson in the Garden, as it became clear that this young 6'5" Cincinnati guard was the real deal.[i] Today, the single-game scoring record in Madison Square Garden is 62—only six points more than Robertson's record back then.

After his performance in New York, the entire nation got to know Oscar Robertson's name because it was all over the press. Different newspapers only had wonderful things to say about this college sophomore who, just two years ago, was leading Crispus Attucks to two state titles in high school. Different people after that 1958 game in the Garden were declaring him as someone who had the makings of the greatest player of all time. They were not wrong because, at that time, not even the best players in the NBA could put up the numbers that Robertson was putting up in college.

Oscar Robertson became an even bigger name when he dominated St. Joseph with 43 points. Since then, he became so popular that kids would watch him warm up before games. All of the Bearcats' games, home or away, were sold out because people wanted to watch him play. He became an icon in basketball because of what he did in New York. And that continued until the rest of his basketball career.

As big of a star as Robertson was, he quickly realized that not even the best players in the country could escape the curse of racism. In one of their road games in Texas, he was forced to stay in a college dorm because the hotel that the team had chosen to stay would not allow him to stay there. He was by far the team's best player, as none of his other teammates even came close to what he could do on the floor. But that was not enough for the hotel to welcome him into their doors with open arms.

In the game that followed after that experience, Robertson scored a season-low of 13 points because he could not sleep that night due to the bad experience. He told George Smith that he would never want to be away from the team ever again because of the experience that he had.

In spite of it all, Robertson powered his team to the conference championship after leading his team to a comeback win when they trailed by nine in the final ten minutes of their game against Wichita. Winning the conference title meant that they were qualified as one of the 16 teams to play in the NCAA Tournament. The rules back then stated that only the team that won its respective conference title would be able to qualify. As such, even the second-best team in the nation would not qualify if it does not win its respective conference championship.

In the first round of the NCAA Tournament, Robertson and the Bearcats faced a Kansas State team coached by the legendary Tex Winter, the man who would be credited for revolutionizing the triangle offense: the same kind of offense that allowed Michael Jordan to win six NBA championships and Kobe Bryant to win five. His team managed to beat Robertson and Cincinnati in overtime after Robertson had fouled out of the game early in the extra period. Despite the loss, Cincinnati still had to play another game against a fellow losing team for the sake of determining their respective places in the tournament. Robertson, still bitter from his loss against Kansas State, dominated Arkansas for 56 points and 10 assists. But the win was a consolation prize that did not matter in the larger scheme of things for him.

During his sophomore year in college, Robertson was named a consensus All-American. He averaged ridiculous numbers of 35.1 points and 15.2 rebounds while shooting 57% from the field the entire season. It was true that he was indeed the nation's best sophomore. And considering that Wilt Chamberlain decided to skip his senior year in college, Robertson eventually became the nation's best player during his junior season.

The Cincinnati Royals, during the spring of that year, took the chance of drafting Robertson under the NBA's territorial rule, which allowed a team to draft a college player playing for a team within a 50-mile radius from their home arena as long as that team forfeits its first-round pick. Robertson's future was already sealed when the Royals chose him in 1958, but he did not mind what they did because he was focused on the two years he had remaining in college.

Before his junior season in college, Robertson was offered a chance to play for the Harlem Globetrotters, a basketball team that was basically playing to entertain people instead of actually competing hard. However, Chamberlain became the team's meal ticket when he skipped his final year in college to play with the Globetrotters for a huge sum of $65,000.

However, Robertson was offered a sum of $17,000. He understood why. He was never as flashy as the rest of the Globetrotters because his game was more fundamentally sound. But the Globetrotters wanted him because they needed a big-name player to sell tickets. Chamberlain was that guy for them, but he was about to go to the NBA in 1959. Still, The Big O refused the offer because he was succeeding in college as a player and as a student. Finishing college and making his way to the NBA after his four-year stint was much better than playing for the Globetrotters for $17,000 a year. He had never heard from the Globetrotters since then.[i]

Robertson, heading into his junior year in college, knew that he was going to be a marked man because teams saw just how good he was during his sophomore year. Knowing that opposing teams would throw different defenses at him, he began experimenting with his personal drills. He asked different athletes, such as pole vaulters and those with solid builds, to try to guard him near the basket so that he could work on different ways of finishing his shots. The idea was that if he had gotten used to finishing against different types of athletes, it would become second nature to him in an actual game setting.

However, no amount of training could prepare him for what he experienced in North Carolina when the team went there for a three-game holiday tournament called the Dixie Classic. Of course, considering the situation in the south, Robertson was not allowed to stay in a hotel. That was why the entire team stayed in a college dorm during the entire tournament.

Then, during the games, Oscar Robertson had the worst experience of his college career at that point in time when he could hear racial slurs, insults, and curses from the crowd. On top of that, the teams that defended him physically were given a great deal of leeway by the referees. Whenever Robertson was on the sidelines, all sorts of objects were being thrown at him. The Bearcats ended up losing two of their three games during that tournament.

After one of the games, George Smith went over to the official's office to let them hear what he had to say. Following his outburst, he went over to Robertson to comfort and hug him with tears rolling down his eyes. That was when Oscar realized that Smith's heart was in the right place and that he genuinely cared for his player.[i]

Despite that experience, there were also memorable experiences that allowed Robertson to feel happy knowing that there were plenty of people who appreciated him as a person. In Denton, Texas, where the team was once again forced to stay in a University dorm, a lady in a restaurant told Oscar that she and the people over in Nashville, Tennessee were proud of him because they knew that he was born among them. Meanwhile, after a tough game, he refused to sign an autograph for a kid but was convinced by one of his teammates to do so. The child told him that he was welcome to join them in church anytime.[i]

Despite all of the hatred surrounding black people during that era, Robertson was happy that the few people who appreciated him and were proud of him had been more than enough to make up for all of the racial slurs and insults that were thrown at him in places where black people were not welcome.

Robertson endured a singularly bad experience with a reporter from a well-known sports publication that twisted his words in an article. Still, that did not stop him from seeing the good things in other people who he truly trusted. On top of that, he continued to dominate on the court because that was the only place where the craziness of the world struggled to reach. He took his team on a return trip to the NCAA Tournament where in the first round, he finished with 34 points and 10 rebounds to make it to the Elite Eight. The Bearcats were then set for a rematch against Kansas State in what was supposed to be a revenge game for Robertson after the loss they suffered a year ago. This time, he secured a tight win without having to rely on the game going into overtime because of a missed free throw. Against Kansas State, he finished with a triple-double effort of 24 points, 17 rebounds, and 13 assists.

Even though the Bearcats were able to make it to the Final Four, Pete Newell, the head coach of the California Golden Bears, decided that his team was not going to lose to Cincinnati because of a dominant performance from Robertson. He decided to throw double teams at him the entire game, as Robertson finished with only 19 points in a tough outing that saw him shooting 5 out of 19 from the field. Of course, when Robertson was not doing well, the team lost, and the same thing happened against Cal in that game.

That loss meant that Robertson was only a few wins shy of a National Championship. The Cincinnati Bearcats finished the season ranked fifth in the entire nation, as he averaged 32.6 points, 16.3 rebounds, and 6.9 assists in his junior year in college. He was once again a Consensus All-American and was no doubt the best individual player in the college ranks.

But being the best player in the nation did not mean anything for Oscar Robertson because, right after the National Tournament, his mother was rushed to the hospital for surgery, having suffered a kidney infection. While the operation was successful, Oscar was hurt because she had to go into debt due to the huge hospital bills. He could not do anything at that time because NBA rules prohibited players from entering the league before their college class graduated. That meant that he had to stay in Cincinnati for one more year, whether he wanted to or not. And he willed through his final year in college with his mother as his source of strength because he did not want her to ever work a single day in her life again.

During Robertson's senior year, his team was ranked the favorite to win the National Championship—the only thing that he was yet to win in college. True enough, thanks to his dominance, Robertson was able to showcase why the Bearcats were the favorites to win it all that season. There were some teams that came close to doing so, but no team ever defeated them in their first ten games, as Robertson's lowest outing in those first ten games was a 25-point performance. He even put up 50 against Iowa in New York.

While the Bearcats lost a game after 13 straight wins, Robertson ended up becoming the all-time leader in points scored in college when he scored a layup against Drake on February 1, 1960. This was a record he held until Pete Maravich broke it a few years later. He currently stands at 11th all-time in points scored in college, but he played during a time when freshmen were not allowed to suit up for the varsity team. Save for Maravich, all of the other players who ended up scoring more career points than Robertson played all four years in college.

Oscar Robertson was not done because he played the game of his life against North Texas, who had the nation's fifth-leading scorer (Oscar was first). He showed that he was miles ahead of the opposing team's best player when he finished the game with 62 points. Robertson broke the conference record for most points scored in a single game.

Thanks to Robertson's efforts, the Cincinnati Bearcats entered the NCAA Tournament with only one loss during the entire regular season. They breezed through the first two rounds, with The Big O scoring 72 total points in those two games. Then came the Final Four when the Bearcats had to face Pete Newell and California once again. This was the very same team that employed a defense that Robertson could not solve a year ago.

Newell said that his game plan was focused on reducing the damage that Robertson could make. As Cal was not a team that had plenty of great scorers and terrific athletes, Newell employed a slow-paced half-court offense that minimized possessions so that The Big O could not maximize the damage that he could make. On top of that, whenever the Bearcats were on offense, Newell sent two or three guys to defend Robertson.

An undersized Bearcats team could not stop the slow-paced half-court offense that Cal used to methodically score against Cincinnati's smaller frontline. Newell once again defeated Robertson's Bearcats and limited the nation's best player to 18 points. Meanwhile, in the National Finals, Ohio State had the size to beat California for the championship. Ohio State sophomore standout Jerry Lucas, Robertson's future longtime teammate, won the only award that The Big O missed out on during his entire college career.

Robertson finished his college career averaging 33.7 points, 14.1 rebounds, and 7.3 assists. He also won the Player of the Year award for the third straight year in his stellar college career. It was indeed true that a championship was the only thing that he missed out on in his four-year stay with Cincinnati. Unfortunately, he never won a championship for Cincinnati in both the collegiate and the professional ranks.

After his senior year, Robertson's jersey number, 12, was retired and was never worn again. He was undoubtedly the best player the program has ever produced, especially with the stellar numbers and performances he had in his career with the Bearcats. And what was most important for him was that people wanted to play for Cincinnati because of Robertson's tenure with a team that was never known for being great at basketball.

Robertson graduated from the University of Cincinnati in 1960 with a degree in business administration. He may have had a rough start and some tough times during his stay there, but he did end up having a stellar basketball career and a good education that became invaluable to him after his playing career in the NBA was over. Of course, the friends and connections he made in college proved to be just as invaluable as his education as well.

However, Robertson's college days were now over. It was now time for the best player in the collegiate ranks to make his way to the NBA, where he soon became one of the league's best players. The dream was about to come true for Oscar because being in the NBA allowed him to earn enough for himself and his family so that all of the sacrifices his parents made for him would be paid back tenfold. This boy who grew up on a Tennessee farm to a poor black family was now going to be one of the biggest names in the history of the sport of basketball.

Chapter 4: NBA Career

Before The Rookie Year

Before Robertson joined the Cincinnati Royals, the team was desperately struggling. The franchise that is now called the Sacramento Kings had just relocated to Cincinnati in 1957, during Robertson's sophomore year in college. And the worst part was that they had to suffer one of the worst injuries in NBA history when Maurice Stokes, a three-time All-Star, was diagnosed with post-traumatic encephalopathy, an illness that prevented him from properly controlling his muscles. This happened due to an accident in a game when his head slammed the floor hard.

Since Stokes' career-ending injury, the Royals struggled. They had former Laker Clyde Lovellette for a single season but forced his way out of Cincinnati because he did not want to play in that city. Since Lovellette left the team, the Royals had only won 38 games from 1958 to 1960. A good duo of Jack Twyman and Wayne Embry was insufficient to give them enough wins. Because of this, the Royals also struggled at the box office because they could not sell tickets. More people were willing to watch the Bearcats, as Robertson's college team was constantly selling out tickets during his stay there. On the other hand, no one wanted to watch the Royals. They could only get about 1,500 fans per game during the seasons prior to The Big O's arrival.

The good thing for the Royals was that they were able to make use of the supplemental territorial draft, which allowed a team to forego their first-round pick that season to select an underclassman that played within 50 miles from their home arena. Considering that the Royals were playing close to the Bearcats, the Royals immediately drafted Robertson in 1958 using their territorial draft rights. Robertson's rights had already belonged to the Royals, even though he still had two more years in college after he was drafted.

However, practically no one wanted to play in Cincinnati. The team drafted Robertson's old college rival, Bob Boozer, with the first pick of the 1959 NBA Draft. But he decided to play for a different team in a different league instead of suiting up for the Royals that season. The Royals had every reason to move away from Cincinnati because they were not winning or even making any money. But they stayed there because they still owned the rights to Robertson, who they thought could turn their franchise around and allow the Royals to make more money. Leaving Cincinnati meant that they would also lose The Big O. Before Robertson signed with the Royals, he had to make sure that he could sway his contract to his favor. That was when Jake Brown, the attorney that convinced him to go to Cincinnati four years ago, spoke with the Royals' front office to discuss the terms of Robertson's contract. And while the league's teams were not yet used to talking to representatives and agents, things were different in this case because the Royals did not want to lose Robertson like they did Boozer a year ago.

By the time the contract negotiations were over, Robertson was set to make $33,000, which was more than six times the average annual salary of most Americans during the 60s. Even though $33,000 would be equal to only about $300,000 today, where most star players make $50 million a year, that was still more than enough for any American back then. Moreover, The Big O's contract also made him the highest-paid player in the history of the NBA, as he surpassed Wilt Chamberlain's $30,000 salary, which the seven-footer earned a year prior.[i]

On top of Robertson's record-breaking salary, he was also set to make money from ticket sales. The commission he was going to make from the tickets pushed his yearly sum to nearly $50,000. His contract also included two additional clauses that became important parts of most NBA contracts today. First, he was going to get paid even if he got injured. And the second was that he could not be traded without his consent.

After the Cincinnati Royals advanced him $15,000, Oscar took care of all of his mother's debt and allowed her to have some extra money so that she could spend more time with her church choir instead of working multiple jobs. He had already fulfilled his dreams of taking care of his mother. Now, all he needed to do was to take care of his NBA career so that he could continue to play the game he loves at the highest possible level.

The Big O Dominates As A Rookie

Before the season started, Robertson got wind of what Bob Cousy, the NBA's greatest point guard at that time, had said about him. Cousy believed that Jerry West, also a rookie, was going to be better than Robertson. But Oscar did not think anything of it because he respected what Bob Cousy had done to the sport of basketball and as a pioneer for the point guard spot. On top of that, Robertson respected West, whom he became friends with during their multiple meetings in college and when they became co-captains of the 1960 Olympic basketball team.

Despite Jerry West being white, Oscar Robertson never felt that he was treated differently by the man that would soon become the model of the NBA's logo. They both had something in common, and that was the fact that they were born in smaller towns and had humble upbringings. This allowed them to develop a sense of humility that they carried throughout their respective careers. They also had nicknames for one another. Oscar called Jerry "Zeke" because of his nickname "Zeke from Cabin Creek." Meanwhile, West called Robertson "Donut" because The Big O resembles a donut. As such, even though the players and the media were hyping them as rivals heading into their rookie years in the NBA, the friendship that they cultivated before they got to the big league allowed them to develop a healthy respect for one another. And this healthy respect turned into a rivalry that never became personal between the two guards that would help shape the playmaker position in the NBA.

Oscar Robertson played his first official NBA game against Jerry West and the Los Angeles Lakers that season. He finished the game with his first career triple-double when he had 21 points, 12 rebounds, and 10 assists. That was when the papers knew that he was legit. Everyone in the country soon realized that Robertson was going to be one of the greatest players ever after that victory he had over the Lakers.

Of course, Robertson was not a one-man crew that season. Bob Boozer had decided to play for Cincinnati after a one-year stint in a different league. Meanwhile, the duo of Jack Twyman and Wayne Embry were great targets for his passes because they could both finish whenever they were open. Twyman, for instance, ended up having his most efficient shooting seasons while playing with Robertson because all he had to do was to find his spot and shoot the ball when he got the pass. Prior to playing with The Big O, he had to manufacture his own shots and was often forcing them.

Robertson, as an NBA player, also got to play his natural position as a point guard. In college, he was one of the forwards on the team because Cincinnati had a small lineup that needed him at the frontcourt so that he could rebound and defend. However, in the NBA, the Royals had a good enough frontcourt that Robertson was able to return to his natural position as the primary playmaker and ball-handler. He was always someone who started from the top of the key, where he could see the entire floor and make plays for his teammates when driving to the basket.

The confidence as a rookie was also oozing from Robertson. He did not have a rough time adjusting to the NBA because he was confident enough in his knowledge of the game or his skills as a player. Jerry West often joked that The Big O was not a rookie because he did not seem to have a hard time adjusting to the big league. And, at one point, Robertson scored 44 on the Philadelphia Warriors and even finished with a triple-double.

When reporters asked him about the fact that he drove on the Warriors and finished a strong layup over Wilt Chamberlain, he said that his confidence was the key and that someone who did not have the confidence to score against arguably the greatest shot blocker in NBA history had no business playing the game of basketball. And this confidence was more than enough for Oscar to get through his rookie year.

Jerry West was right when he said that Robertson was not a rookie because he did not play like one. That season, he was consistently scoring 30 or more points on a nightly basis. He also scored 40 or more points nine times during his rookie season. And triple-doubles, which were rare for any player back then, became commonplace for him.

Robertson finished his rookie season averaging 30.5 points, 10.1 rebounds, and a league-leading 9.7 assists per game. He broke Bob Cousy's record of assists in a single season, as the Houdini of the Hardwood had led the league in assists per game for eight straight seasons. Robertson's ability to see the floor at 6'5" and attract defenders with his scoring allowed him to become the great playmaker that he was.

Triple-doubles became natural for Robertson because he was basically doing everything for the Royals. Back then, double-doubles were normal for NBA players because they could score well and also rebound in bunches. Rebounds were particularly easy to collect because the pace was much faster, and players were not as skilled at finishing as athletes today. That meant that there were going to be plenty of misses that the players could rebound. As such, it was normal for teams to have three players averaging double-digits in rebounds.

However, because of the same fact that not everyone was great at finishing baskets, it was difficult for playmakers to collect assists. That meant that triple-doubles were extremely difficult for players to achieve, as double-digit assists were rare. Then again, due to the fact that he had the size to rebound, the skills to score, and the ability to attract defenders and make plays, Robertson was the very definition of an all-around player that could do it all on the floor.

Due to the revolutionary way he played the game, Oscar Robertson was named the Rookie of the Year in 1961 and was also an All-Star in his first season in the NBA (becoming the All-Star Game MVP). While Cincinnati failed to make the playoffs, the future was bright because attendance was much better. And they also went on to improve their record that season and nearly made the playoffs.

The First Triple-Double Season in NBA History

The 1961-62 season was one of the strangest and biggest seasons in the history of the NBA because of how it marked a lot of firsts. That was the year that Chicago joined the league. Of course, the Boston Celtics remained as dominant as ever and went on to become the first team in league history to win 60 games—an achievement that two or three teams end up doing every single season in today's modern NBA.

But the fact that the Celtics did that back in the day was a huge achievement because of the circumstances. Traveling from one city to another was not as easy as it is today because teams had to travel by road or through regular flight schedules instead of flying on a chartered flight or in private jets. Moreover, every team had to face one another about 10 or so times in a single season, and that made it easier for teams to memorize each squad's plays or to understand each player's tendencies.

Oscar Robertson used to say that you could interchange a team's starting five with another, and both teams would still be able to run each other's offensive systems because they had gotten so used to playing against each other that they already memorized their sets and tendencies. And the fact that everyone memorized each team's plays meant that it was going to be more difficult to get a win over a team that knows each other so well. This meant that the 60-win season that the Celtics had that year was such an achievement. There was also the fact that this was the season wherein Wilt Chamberlain averaged 50 points a night and was able to score 100 points in a single season—a record that is yet to be toppled by any of the immensely talented players in the NBA today. Chamberlain was so dominant throughout the early part of his career that he led the league in scoring through his first seven seasons. And it is difficult to overstate just how great Wilt was, even if we were to factor in how he was physically and fundamentally leagues away from most of the other centers in the league.

It is also noteworthy that Oscar Robertson himself had a season that was just as statistically ridiculous as any other season in the history of the NBA. He may not have been in the same area as Wilt in terms of his dominance, but The Big O did things his own way, which was basically him doing everything else at a high level. And he achieved something that no one in the history of the league had ever done before that season.

Robertson continued to dominate the NBA as a second-year player by doing everything he could possibly do. He scored, rebounded, and made plays for others. That was why, through his first four games, he had four straight triple-double performances. The highlight was when he had 22 assists against the Syracuse Nationals on October 29, 1961.

The triple-double became something of a norm for Oscar Robertson that season because he was the one who was responsible for setting his team up for open shots if he could not score the ball himself. And considering that he was one of the biggest and most athletic players on his team, rebounding came naturally for him to the point that it became normal for him to rebound the ball in bunches as well. As a matter of fact, he finished that season with 41 triple-doubles, and that meant that he had triple-doubles in more than half of the 79 games that he played in his second year in the league. Robertson was always a great scorer and rebounder in all of the levels of basketball that he played. Even though he was already a great passer during his high school and college years, putting up double-digit assist games did not come quite as easy before he became pro because the teammates he had in the past were not as great at finishing passes as NBA players are. And an assist today is much easier to get back in the 60s because NBA stats people tend to be a bit generous in handing out assists in the modern version of the game.

Still, at the end of the 1961-62 season, Robertson achieved what was seemingly impossible at that time when he averaged 30.8 points, 12.5 rebounds, and 11.4 assists to become the first player to average a triple-double in a single season. This also marked the first time in league history that the league's assist leader averaged double digits in assists. And his triple-double feat was something that he did not consciously try to achieve back then because no one thought that the triple-double was a big deal during those days.

The history of the triple-double is not something that has been widely explored. During Magic Johnson's years of dominance in the 1980s, he was the triple-double king that could put up all-around stats at any given moment. But he did not average a triple-double in a single season, even though he came close to doing so twice. The NBA was on a rising trajectory during the 80s partly because of the excitement that Johnson brought to the league and because of his rivalry with the Boston Celtics' Larry Bird.

Of course, the media would try to do anything to make Magic Johnson into someone larger than life by pulling out all of the stats possible and by making the triple-double something that was just as larger than life as the Lakers point guard. Magic was someone known for doing everything possible out on the floor to the point that people believed that he was the best at compiling all-around stats. This was during the 80s when no one could go on the internet to type "triple-double leader in the NBA" in a search bar. People had to dig through books and sheets to look at the stats of the players that played during the earlier years of the NBA.[i] That was when they found out that Oscar Robertson was doing something in the 60s that not even the great Magic Johnson had been able to do in his prime, which was to average a triple-double in a single season. And the most surprising thing was that

Robertson was not doing that because he was consciously aware of his numbers or that he knew that he would look good to the media if he was putting up those stats.

Today's NBA players are always conscious of how many points, rebounds, and assists they have. A player could easily look up to the jumbotron to see his numbers. There are also some players that could go to the bench and pull up a smartphone or tablet to look at stats. There have been cases where a player would deliberately do an odd play or ask one of his teammates to give him a rebound just so he could achieve a triple-double. And when a player achieves that stat even for just one game, the performance becomes a media sensation.

The only other NBA player in history to ever average a triple-double was Russell Westbrook, who first achieved it in 2017 and went on to average that stat line four times in his entire career. But, with all due respect to Westbrook, he was conscious of the fact that he had the opportunity to chase history every single time he was close to a triple-double in the games that he played. And when it became clear that he could sustain averaging a triple-double in an entire season, he went for it because he knew that he wanted to achieve it and that he could do it.

That is the same case for most players who have become good enough to put up triple-doubles on a regular basis. They are aware of the stats because it is so easy to know how many points, rebounds, and assists they have. Winning the game is still the priority. But if a player knows that he can make his victory look so much better on paper, especially if he is close to a triple-double, he would actually go for it.

Records are made to be broken, and the players today know about the records that have been set in the past because it is so easy for someone to educate himself about the numbers that were achieved long ago and about the people who put up those ridiculous numbers. But that was not the case for Oscar Robertson and the people who played during his era. Robertson averaged a triple-double not because he was consciously aware of it but because he just did. It was part of his game to do everything, which included scoring, rebounding, and playmaking. Averaging a triple-double was not something he kept track of every night because a triple-double was not even something that was used as a measure of a player's greatness back then. Those were just numbers that Robertson was able to achieve as a slave of the moment instead of as someone who was perfectly conscious of his stats. This may bring to mind Willie Mays, a baseball legend who commented on what Jose Canseco was able to achieve back in the 80s as the first man to hit forty home runs and steal 40 bases in one season. Mays said that he could have done it during his time if he knew that it would have become such a big deal. He even went on to say that he could have actually done a 50-50 if he knew that it was going to be celebrated.[iv]

Oscar Robertson was always a confident player, but he was never someone who would boisterously say that he could have averaged a triple-double more than once or twice his entire career'. It tends to be different when someone has a direct goal in mind and when a player wants to achieve certain stats as opposed to when a player is simply doing what he can to contribute and win. Robertson was the latter throughout his entire career.

Then again, to be able to sustain a triple-double or to play at an excellent all-around level throughout an entire career is something that not a lot of people could do in their career. Robertson had the skills and gifts necessary for that.

He was big, fast, and strong. But the most important aspect that led to him averaging a triple-double was his understanding of the game. Understanding the game is the crucial element when it comes to knowing when to make the right pass and knowing where and how to position for a rebound.

Robertson said it himself when he remarked that the game was just as mental as physical. Everyone needs a certain level of understanding to achieve a level of excellence and to sustain it throughout an entire season. That very same basketball IQ separates an elite player from a great athlete who is just a tad below stardom. And not even the most gifted athletes can trump a player who possesses a good combination of skill and basketball IQ.[i]

At the end of the first triple-double season—an achievement that stood as the one and only of its kind for 55 years, Robertson led his team to 43 wins to qualify for the playoffs. However, the Royals could only win a game against the Detroit Pistons in their playoff matchup. The Big O averaged 28.8 points, 11 rebounds, and 11 assists in his four-game series against Detroit.

And despite his amazing season during the 1961-62 campaign, he did not win the MVP award. But not even Wilt Chamberlain won the award after averaging 50 points and 25 rebounds the entire season. Robertson finished third behind the two biggest stars of the 60s—Bill Russell and Wilt Chamberlain.

Bill Russell did not average gaudy numbers when compared to what Robertson and Chamberlain were doing. But he was the unquestioned leader and driving force of a dominant Boston Celtics team that eventually won the 1962 NBA championship. It was clear that, as early as the 60s, the MVP was always given to the best player on the best team.

The following year was a bit uneventful for Robertson and the Cincinnati Royals, as far as their basketball performance was concerned, because the makeup of the team did not change a lot. Cincinnati won 42 games during the regular season; meanwhile, Robertson nearly averaged another triple-double after finishing the 1962-63 season with 28.3 points, 10.4 rebounds, and 9.5 assists. The rise of other players, such as Wayne Embry and Bob Boozer, made it possible for him to contribute without having to put up ridiculous stats every single night.

While the team was not as good as they were a year prior in terms of their wins in the regular season, the Royals were able to pull off a first-round upset over the higher-seeded Syracuse Nationals in the first round. It was Oscar Robertson who paved the way for his first-ever series win in the playoffs when he managed to compile 29.4 points, 13.8 rebounds, and 9.6 assists in that five-game series. And he ended the final two games of that series, both of which were wins, with triple-doubles.

When the team owner of the Royals passed away in 1963, there was confusion in the front office because several people wanted to buy the team from the estate. The team's ownership changed hands a few times during that time, but neither Robertson nor the Royals cared about it because they had to do their job on the court against the four-time defending champions. They were going to face the Boston Celtics in the second round.[i] Entering that round, the Royals were the clear underdogs that no one gave a shot against the most dominant team in league history at that point or quite possibly ever. But Oscar Robertson did not care about it because he had to bring his best against the best. He was facing Bill Russell, who he recognized as the best player in the league because of his defensive impact and the way he led his team with his intangibles. Oscar and Wilt may have been the more impressive players when it comes to their stats, but Bill was someone that everyone needed to see in person to understand why he was the best.

Despite playing the best team and the best player, Robertson led his team from a massive deficit and stormed away with a win in Game 1. He was the one who led the comeback win over the defending champions by going for 43 points, 14 rebounds, and 10 assists in that victory. But Boston came back in Game 2 to take a blowout win over Cincinnati.

When the Royals defeated the Celtics in Game 3, they were up 2-1. The momentum was on the side of the underdogs who no one thought had a chance to beat the team that had won the last four NBA championships. But everything changed when the Royals returned to Cincinnati for Game 4, where they found out that their new owner had booked the Cincinnati Gardens for the circus throughout the entire playoffs, even though he was aware that the team had made the postseason. This meant that the Royals had to temporarily relocate to Xavier University's arena, which was very small compared to the already small Cincinnati Gardens.[i]

Boston went on to win the game against Cincinnati in their temporary arena by 18 points, as Oscar Robertson had one of his worst shooting games. And despite a triple-double output in Game 5, Robertson could not salvage his team in Boston, as the Celtics ended up winning that game to take control of the series.

Despite playing in a different arena, Robertson was not willing to lose in Game 6 because he wanted to extend the season as far back as he could. That was when he poured in 36 points, 15 rebounds, and 14 assists in that game. The Royals were able to push the series to a seventh and deciding game. It seemed like they had the defending champions' number.

Game 7 was different because that was when Bob Cousy of the Celtics took control, not knowing whether or not that would be his final game. Regardless of what the outcome of that season would be, he was going to retire at the end of it. And that meant that he had nothing to lose as he orchestrated the Boston offense to perfection and was hitting big shots. Even though Robertson outplayed him with his 43 points, Cousy was the better point guard with the better team that season. The Celtics defeated the Royals in an 11-point win, as Robertson had to go back to the drawing board. But he received a lot of praise from Bill Russell, who said that he was happy that they won because he had already seen too much of Oscar Robertson. And even though Cousy had his issues with Robertson in the past, he also had high praises for the younger point guard when he said that Sam Jones, who defended Oscar throughout the entire series, was happy that they were already out of that series.[i]

Joining NBA Royalty, Falling Short

The Royals were already good enough to give the Boston Celtics a scare, despite having a roster that relied almost entirely on Robertson. However, they were able to acquire Jerry Lucas, one of the greatest rebounders in the history of the game. Lucas was originally drafted in 1962 by the Royals. However, due to contractual issues, he did not suit up during the 1962-63 season. It was only during the 1963-64 season that Lucas decided to go to the NBA, despite the fact that he did not want to play in Cincinnati. He did not have a choice, however, because the Royals held his rights. And while he and the Royals front office did not agree on a lot of different things, the franchise did not have a choice because Cincinnati could not afford to lose a player of Lucas's caliber.

With Jerry Lucas teaming up Wayne Embry and Bob Boozer on the frontcourt, the Cincinnati Royals became very dangerous heading into the 1963-64 season. The team also had a new coach in Jack McMahon, who was one of the fiercest coaches in the league. He was as intense and fiery as any coach could get. But, as a former player himself, he knew how to balance scolding his players and knowing how to be nice and easy on them because he knew what it was like being on the receiving end of a scolding from a coach.

Like a lot of different teams with talented players, the Royals saw a few problems at the start because Jerry Lucas was used to having the ball in his hands from the post. He was always a talented player from the post, as he set records in college with his field goal shooting accuracy. Lucas knew how to finish and was used to operating from the post in almost every offensive set. But that was not the case for him when he joined the Royals.

The Royals relied on Robertson's ability to break defenses down, and that was why he always had the ball in his hands. But The Big O was never selfish. He always found a way to incorporate his teammates into the offense. Lucas struggled to adjust to having a point guard setting him up for his points instead of finding scoring opportunities from the post. That was what led to the false reports that he and Robertson did not get along.[i] But the truth was that they both respected one another.

Nevertheless, having one more player that could score and rebound effectively gave the Royals more depth at the frontcourt, especially when they had to go up against other frontcourts that were just as talented and deep. That also meant that Oscar Robertson had one more player that he could dish the ball to whenever he was driving to the basket, and Lucas eventually adjusted to a style wherein all he had to do was to learn when to move and cut to get an easy basket from his talented point guard.

Thanks to how well the star players on the team adjusted, the Royals began to make some noise and even went on to go on a run that allowed them to trail only the Celtics for the best record. It was thanks to how McMahon allowed both Lucas and Embry to play from the post so that Robertson could find openings down at the middle of the defense.

By the end of the regular season, Robertson narrowly missed averaging another triple-double when he finished the campaign with a personal career-high of 31.4 points, 9.9 rebounds, and 11 assists. He was a few rebounds shy of averaging ten, which, had it mattered at the time, would have given him another triple-double season. The only reason why Robertson did not average double digits in rebounding was the fact that they had Lucas dominating the rebounds. Oscar needed to rebound well in the past to help his frontcourt teammates but no longer needed to crash the boards as hard as he once did when Lucas began clearing the rebounds for the team.

While he may not have averaged a triple-double, Robertson still ended the season as the league's Most Valuable Player. He was named the MVP for the first and only time in his NBA career not only because he had ridiculous stats, but also because he led the Cincinnati Royals to the second seed in the East with a total of 55 wins. Robertson was always great at piling up crazy statistics but struggled to attain a lot of wins in the regular season. But now that he had a lot of wins on his side, the narrative shifted to his favor, as voters believed that he was indeed the best player on one of the best teams in the NBA. Robertson actually finished with the largest margin of victory for the MVP award at that point in NBA history. And to top it all off, Jerry Lucas was named the Rookie of the Year.

Oscar Robertson was actually surprised after winning the MVP award because he never thought about winning it. It was normal for any player to think about not winning the MVP award during the 60s because it usually went to a center. And the players that were synonymous with the center position during the 60s were Bill Russell and Wilt Chamberlain.

It was not a surprise that nine of the ten MVP awards during the 60s went to either Bill or Wilt. After all, they were the faces of the NBA because they symbolized what basketball was all about—two gigantic figures that were larger than life squaring off for a championship year after year. And the only time a player other than either Russell or Chamberlain was able to win the MVP was when Robertson did so in 1964, proving that he belonged to the conversation as arguably the third-best player behind the two centers that dominated the league during the 60s. But while the Royals finished with a good record, Robertson believed in hindsight that they did not have what it took to maintain their pace when the playoffs were fast approaching.[i] That was because the team had previously traded Bob Boozer, who had gone from being the third or fourth option to fifth or six. While Boozer did not play at the level of an All-Star, his size and versatility added depth to the Royals' frontcourt. They did not have that depth entering the playoffs.

The Royals struggled to put away the newly relocated Philadelphia 76ers (formerly the Syracuse Nationals) because Robertson felt that their big men had become too weary. They still defeated the Nationals, but it took them all of the five games that were given to them in the first round to defeat a team that had only won 34 games during the regular season.

When it was time for the Royals to face the Celtics in a rematch of last season's second round, Cincinnati had run out of gas. Boston did not need to focus a lot of their defensive attention on the tired Cincinnati frontcourt.

Instead, they keyed in on Robertson, who they limited to 28.2 points on 40% shooting during the entire second round. Boston ended up beating Cincinnati in five games, despite the fact that The Big O enjoyed his best season at that point in his career.

If there was something that both Robertson and Lucas regretted in their entire careers, it was that they never won a championship for Cincinnati during their days there. Those back-to-back second-round meetings with the Boston Celtics were the closest they ever got. But while both Robertson and Lucas ended up winning titles, later on, it was such a shame that they never won together while they were still in Cincinnati. The only time the Royals ever won a championship was in 1951, when they were still in Rochester.

A year later, the Royals did not change their roster makeup except for the addition of Happy Hairston, who went on to fill some of the holes left by Bob Boozer. However, the team failed to perform up to par compared to how good everyone was during the 1963-64 season. And an even bigger problem was the fact that Wayne Embry and Jack Twyman were no longer performing at the same level that they used to. Despite that, the Royals had a one-two punch in Robertson and Lucas, who both went on to become superstars and an early version of the inside-outside duo that eventually became a staple in championship teams. However, the Royals were not championship contenders, even though they did have a lineup that looked like it could win a championship on paper.

During the 1964-65 season, the Royals won 48 games to make the playoffs. Robertson finished the season narrowly missing another triple-double average when he finished with numbers of 30.4 points, 9 rebounds, and a new career-high of 11.5 assists. Through his first five seasons in the NBA, The Big O averaged 30.4 points, 10.4 rebounds, and 10.6 assists to become the only player to average a triple-double through the first five seasons of his career.

But while Robertson did indeed have a great season, the Royals could not perform up to par in the postseason. During the playoffs, they were completely dominated by a Wilt Chamberlain-led Philadelphia 76ers team that took the series in four games. For all his brilliance, Oscar struggled against Wilt's inside presence and averaged 28 points on only 42.7% shooting from the field in that series.

It was after the 1964-65 season that Oscar Robertson's relationship with the Cincinnati Royals front office became sour. This was because his contract was already done and he was expecting to get a good payday, especially with his performance for the team the last five seasons as arguably one of the top three players in the NBA. The problem during the 60s was that when a player was drafted by a team, he was virtually locked in with that franchise his entire life. When a player's contract is done, the only NBA team he can negotiate with is the same team he played for. Players were not allowed to negotiate with other franchises in the NBA, and the only escape they had from a team that they did not want to play for was to get traded or to sign with another league that did not pay as much as an NBA franchise did. In Robertson's case, his only choice was to negotiate with the Royals for a new contract. He was looking to get a good salary because the NBA was already at a better place than it had been five years ago. The league had already acquired a good television deal that improved its profits. On top of that, because larger-than-life superstars such as Wilt Chamberlain, Bill Russell, Jerry West, and Oscar Robertson were becoming more and more popular, the interest in the league was also at an all-time high.

But the problem was that the Royals were trying to low-ball The Big O into taking the same salary he was receiving in his previous contract.[i] In comparison, Wilt Chamberlain and Bill Russell were playing for six-digit contracts. Robertson was only asking for a raise of $10,000; The management did not want to negotiate on the matter. That was when Robertson, throughout the offseason, refused to work with the Royals until he could get a new contract. He even went as far as saying, "They don't seem to want me to play" to reporters. And considering that there was a possibility of him touring the west coast while playing for other basketball teams that allowed him to make enough money, he did consider leaving the NBA.

It was never because Oscar Robertson was greedy. He was a frugal person that valued the worth of every penny he had because he grew up poor. His parents raised him well enough to understand what it meant to work hard without ever complaining about the money. It was not as if Robertson was complaining about what he was getting paid. Instead, it was only that he knew what he was worth. Growing up knowing the value of every penny and working for that money, he knew that he was worth more than what the Royals were willing to pay him. After all, the only reason people were willing to watch the Royals was the fact that Robertson was playing for them. He was not willing to be low-balled into accepting a contract that he believed did not reflect his worth. And by keeping his stance on the matter, he was sticking it into the Royals management that focused more on profits than on keeping the team happy.

A few days before the start of the 1965-66 season, Robertson and the Royals finally settled on a contract that allowed the superstar to stay happy for a while until he realized that the team was not going anywhere with the decisions the front office was making. It was not only the contract disputes with Cincinnati that led to the poor relationship between the Royals and Robertson. The fact that the Royals' management was not doing what was best for the future of the franchise was what ultimately did them in.

During the 1965-66 season, the Cincinnati Royals were still a decent ball club that could contend with just about any other team in the league, especially with the team sporting two superstars in their prime. Robertson could still put up a triple-double at any given moment but was going to cede the rebounding to Lucas, a walking 20-20 player that was probably only third behind Russell and Wilt as a rebounder. But outside of that duo, the team struggled to find consistent performers. As good as he was during his peak, Wayne Embry had regressed due to the wear and tear that NBA players regularly suffered during the 60s when the players were not as well taken care of as they are today. And the Royals did not have a consistent presence near the basket when it came to defense because Embry was already slowing down, and, as good of a rebounder and offensive player as he was, Lucas was not the best defender. In other words, the Royals were placed in a tough situation where all they could do was to try to outscore every team in the league because they could not defend at a consistently competitive level. If they had a bad shooting night, they did not have anything to throw at the opposing team because their defense struggled.

Robertson ended the 1965-66 season averaging 31.3 points, 7.7 rebounds, and 11.1 assists. He was still the engine that drove the Cincinnati offense because of his scoring and playmaking, but the problem was that there was still only so much that he could do as an offensive player when the team was struggling to defend. The Royals went on to finish the season with 45 wins and then marched into the playoffs against the Boston Celtics, who defeated them in five games.

The 1966-67 season was when things truly took a turn for the worse for the Royals. Robertson was still the same old Big O that could score in bunches and make plays for others, but the team just did not have the right pieces. Outside of Jerry Lucas, who had one of his most inefficient seasons due to the lack of other scorers on the team, there was no one that could contribute on a regular basis. The team could still score, but the defense suffered. As a result, the Royals averaged more points allowed than points scored throughout the entire regular season.

That season, the Royals fell to 39 wins but still managed to make it to the playoffs. Then again, Robertson, who averaged more than 30 points and 10 assists for the fourth straight season, did not have enough pieces around him to contend against a Philadelphia 76ers team that had broken the NBA record in terms of total wins in the regular season with 68. Chamberlain became more of a passer at that point in his career, even though he was still a nightly 20-20 player. And due to the amazing team offense that the Sixers played, they dominated the Royals in four games during the 1967 playoffs.

Ever since that terrific 55-game win season that the Royals enjoyed during the 1963-64 season, everything went downhill for them. That was the only chance that Robertson had to win a title in Cincinnati, but the pieces just were not there for the team. On top of that, like many of the other teams in the 60s, they had the Boston Celtics to contend with. And after the 1967 playoffs, it became apparent that things just would not work out for Robertson in Cincinnati, the city he had been playing basketball for since his freshman year in college.

The Final Years In Cincinnati

After the 1967 playoffs, Jack McMahon was fired as the Royals' head coach and was replaced by Ed Jucker, who had won the National Championship for the University of Cincinnati in the two following years after Oscar Robertson had graduated from the school. Jucker coached the team after George Smith had also left following Robertson's graduation. And he went on to win back-to-back titles for the team in 1961 and 1962 without a single player that made it to the NBA. Even though the Bearcats did not have a lot of talented players when Robertson left, he set the standard that the team needed to follow because he was the one who instilled the winning culture in Cincinnati. And that was something that Jucker, as the team's head coach, continued in the two years after The Big O left the program to pursue his NBA career.

But as successful as Ed Jucker may have been in college, the NBA was an entirely different monster. It is not a secret that the best college coaches do not always transition well from college to the NBA, even today. And that was what happened to Jucker during his years as the head coach of the Cincinnati Royals.

Robertson believed that Jucker did not coach the team right. Even though The Big O was always the point guard and the top playmaker of the team, he decided to bring in more playmakers in an attempt to minimize the damage that Robertson was getting from defenders whenever he brought the ball up the court. The team traded for Guy Rodgers, the only other player to lead the league in assists ever since Oscar Robertson entered the NBA in 1960. Rodgers was already older, but he was still a good backup point guard that also played in the backcourt together with Robertson during certain stretches.

Robertson did not think that this was a good idea on the part of Jucker. Allowing different playmakers to share the playmaking duty in college has always been a good idea because college games are not built on the prowess of superstars but are more reliant on systems that allow different players to contribute. The reason is that defenders are not as competitive in college, and that is what allows second-string playmakers to also make plays well enough.

Meanwhile, in the NBA, when in need of a basket against a strong defensive team that can take away any role player's offensive game, the ball should be in the hands of the team's best player. This has always been the case throughout the history of the sport, as players such as Jerry West, Magic Johnson, Larry Bird, Michael Jordan, Kobe Bryant, LeBron James, and Stephen Curry need to have the ball in their hands in the most crucial moments of any game.

In Robertson's words, Jucker did not understand pro basketball at all.[i] He did not know about the cardinal rule of NBA basketball, which is to give the ball to the best player or to the playmaker during the most crucial moments of the game. The system of moving the ball around and allowing different playmakers to dictate the offense can be great on a long-term basis. But Jucker took the ball away from Robertson's hands in the stretches where he should have been asked to take over. On top of that, the new coach also did not understand that the wear and tear of playing more than 80 games a season and the more physical brand of basketball in the NBA had bigger effects on a player's body compared to college. Jucker ran the starters to the ground instead of relying more on his bench. And that forced the best players on the Royals to play sluggishly by the middle of the season.

By the end of the 1967-68 season, the Royals were 39-43 and did not qualify for the playoffs for only the second time in Robertson's NBA career. The

Big O averaged 29.2 points and 9.8 assists, as that was also the first time in the last five seasons that he did not average double digits in assists. And the worst part was that the Royals had the lowest attendance in the entire NBA due to their struggles.

Before the 1968-69 season, Ed Jucker did not think that Robertson would be returning to the team. That was because he had another dispute with the front office regarding a clause in his contract that was not honored well enough by the management of the franchise. The dispute started in 1967 and carried all the way to the 1968 offseason when Robertson's contract was done.[i]

But the Royals finally gave Robertson a three-year contract that was worth nearly $400,000. And what no one expected at that time was that this was the final contract he would ever have with the Royals, as his relationship with that franchise had already reached an all-time low.

The Royals still struggled during the season, especially with Oscar Robertson not reporting to training camp due to his dispute with the management. Of course, at 30 years old, The Big O's legs were not entirely in their best shape. This led to a career-low as a scorer at that point in his career as he averaged 24.7 points, 6.4 rebounds, and 9.8 assists for the Royals. Meanwhile, Cincinnati went on to win 41 games but still could not make the playoffs because the league now had more teams that competed harder than ever'.

After the 1968-69 season, Ed Jucker was removed from his position as the head coach because his success in college could not translate to the NBA. And the entire Royals front office saw a makeover when different personalities from the ownership down to the announcer had fresh faces to usher in what was going to be a new era for the team in an attempt to improve attendance and interest. But the most surprising face that was introduced to the Royals was all-time great point guard Bob Cousy, who revolutionized the playmaker position before Robertson's time. Cousy was already 41 at the time but kept himself in good shape because he still played basketball and other competitive sports from time to time. And he also had coaching experience from when he coached Boston College to the National Tournament. Cousy was not only hired as a coach but also as a player, as playing coaches were becoming common back then, especially with Bill Russell, who had played and coached his final game during the 1969 NBA Finals, coaching the Celtics after Red Auerbach retired. The Royals tried to follow suit by bringing in Cousy as a 41-year old point guard that could help bring in more fans to see Oscar Robertson and the man who was once the greatest point guard in the history of the game.

Initially, Robertson did not mind the Royals bringing in Bob Cousy, even though the older point guard might have said a few things about him in the past. For The Big O, whatever rivalry he and Cousy had was professional and not personal because they were both competitive players. But he did not imagine that he would end up having one of his worst years as a professional in that season under him.

Cousy told the Royals that they lacked discipline and that he needed to work them hard in practice. He wanted them to be like the Celtics, who excelled at running the break almost every single possession. That was when Cousy decided that there were players who did not fit his scheme. He orchestrated a trade that sent Jerry Lucas to San Francisco because he thought that the superstar big man was out of shape. In exchange for Lucas, the Royals received two players who no one today would ever be familiar with because they were not even good enough to become starters. After that, Cousy decided that it was better for Norman Van Lier, an up-and-coming 22-year old rookie point guard, to handle the ball more. This meant that Robertson was not going to be the usual ball-handler he used to be and was forced to play off the ball by coming off of screens and by finishing in the lane. And this was a problem because Van Lier was a lot shorter than Robertson and struggled to see over the top of defenses.

Meanwhile, the original plan that Cousy had was to be a playing coach. However, whenever he inserted himself into the game, he had problems with handling the ball because, at 41, he did not have the same kind of physical abilities he once had. This led to turnovers and bad plays on his part. He eventually decided to never play a game of basketball again because he did not want to tarnish the reputation he built prior to that season with the Royals.[i]

What made things even worse was that Cousy was not able to live up to the promise of rebuilding a younger and fresher team that could run and score. Instead, the Royals had a starting squad composed of players who were already in their 30s. The team's best rebounder was 6'5" Johnny Green, who was already 36 years old that season. And 36 in basketball years during the 60s and early 70s is like 46 in today's game.

Connie Dierking, who was one of their best scorers, was eventually traded, as it was now clear that Cousy was actually trying to rebuild the team from scratch. At times, whenever the team was playing, it did not even look like the Royals had Robertson because there were moments when he did not fit the offense that the new coach was trying to build. He was not using his best player and the man who many regard as the greatest all-around player in league history in the best way possible. And The Big O did not understand what was going on in Cousy's mind because they were not exactly close enough to talk to one another man to man.

Then, in the middle of the season, Robertson was asked by a reporter how he felt about the trade. He was confused about the question, as the reporter was promptly asked to leave. Then Oscar learned from Jake Brown that the Royals had traded him for Gus Johnson, a powerful forward that was once an All-Star but was at the tail end of his career due to having bad knees as a result of all of the jumping he did throughout his career.

After that, Cousy called Robertson to tell him about the trade. He said that the reason for the trade was that he saw that Oscar had become "unhappy" with the team and that the front office decided to ship him over to a contender. The Big O told Cousy to discuss things with Jake Brown, who represented him as his lawyer. And that was when Cousy and the members of the front office found out that Oscar Robertson could veto any trade, as stipulated in his contract.

Brown told them that, since they had already made it public that they were willing to trade Robertson, they should trade him on the condition that Oscar will only be traded to a team he wanted to play for. Baltimore was not that place, and that was when the trade for Gus Johnson was nullified. Robertson needed to think things over first before deciding where he wanted to go.

After a huge media spectacle that saw different writers saying different things about Robertson and various NBA players defending one of the best players of the generation, The Big O finally called a press conference. He told the media that he was going to honor his contract by playing the remaining games of that season and that he was going to be traded to a different team in the offseason. With that, his days in Cincinnati were numbered.

Oscar Robertson played his final game for the Cincinnati Royals on March 21, 1970. In that game, he had 29 points, 11 rebounds, and 7 assists. The game prior to that was the final one he had in front of the Cincinnati crowd, as he went up against his old teammate Jerry Lucas and the San Francisco Warriors. Robertson ended the season averaging 25.3 points, 6.1 rebounds, and 8.1 assists. Those were impressive numbers for a man who was not utilized properly by his coach and was distracted by all of the noise regarding his future with the team. Meanwhile, Cincinnati, having only 36 wins, did not make the playoffs.

The Championship In Milwaukee

While deciding where he wanted to go, Robertson realized the idea of playing in the Midwest was good because of how there were better schools for his children. On top of that, he was born in the Midwest as well. That was when Robertson saw the future of the NBA in Milwaukee when they had a towering figure down in the middle of the paint.

In 1969, the Milwaukee Bucks lucked into the draft when they ended up getting the top overall pick. The Bucks used this pick to draft a 7'2" tower out of UCLA. This man was Lew Alcindor, who was eventually going to be Kareem Abdul-Jabbar, the NBA's all-time leader in career points scored as of this writing. Arguably the greatest center to ever play the game and one of the top five players in the history of the game, Alcindor averaged 28.8 points and 14.5 rebounds during his rookie year.

With Lew in the middle, the Bucks were able to make 56 wins during the regular season. But as good as the future Kareem was, he was outmuscled by

73

the burlier and more experienced 6'9" New York center, Willis Reed, in the playoffs. The Bucks lost in the second round to the Knicks in only five games because they did not have a steady secondary scorer behind Alcindor. They also did not have a point guard that could feed the towering center easy baskets in the paint.

That was when Robertson made his choice. He wanted a chance to play together with a capable superstar that won three straight NCAA championships in college under the legendary John Wooden. Playing in Milwaukee also allowed them to have a change in scenery that was an improvement from the environment back in Cincinnati, where Robertson had already grown accustomed to living but had developed a sour relationship with the management of the Royals.

Robertson was traded to the Milwaukee Bucks for a package that focused on Flynn Robinson, an All-Star guard, and the young Charlie Paulk, who did not last long in the NBA. Still, Bob Cousy thought that Paulk was a find, even though he had not played basketball for nearly two years because he had to finish his military service.

During the 1970-71 season, Cincinnati fell to 33 wins. After that, they fell to 30 wins before the Royals finally relocated to Kansas City during the 1972-73 season. Throughout the next few years after Robertson was traded, the franchise was still poorly handled. Meanwhile, Bob Cousy, who had never coached a playoff team in his entire life, could not even get 40 wins in a single season during his time as an NBA head coach. He finally hung his coaching boots in 1974 as the newly named Kansas City-Omaha Kings were able to finally break their playoff drought under a new coach.

Robertson was in the best situation possible because he could now play for a winning team with younger people that had legs fresh enough for a chance at an NBA title. The last time he was in the playoffs was in 1967, and The Big O was hungry for a championship, the only prize he was yet to win in his illustrious NBA career. The situation in Milwaukee was perfect for Robertson because he had many different teammates that could score at any given moment. Bob Dandridge, a young 23-year old, was on his way to becoming an All-Star. The starting shooting guard, Jon McGlocklin, was a good shooter and was a former All-Star himself. And right down in the middle was Lew Alcindor, who was a year away from becoming Kareem Abdul-Jabbar.

What made Kareem special was the fact that at 7'2", he was already virtually unguardable for most NBA centers that stood several inches shorter. Probably the only player that could physically stand up to his height and length was Wilt Chamberlain, who was already nearing his retirement age when Abdul-Jabbar was dominating the league as a young center. Aside from Wilt, Kareem could shoot over the top of anyone in the league. He was already unstoppable at his height and wingspan. But what made him an even more unstoppable player was his skyhook, a one-legged hook shot that he shot with his shooting arm fully extended in the air. Jumping off of one leg allowed him to gain more elevation. And extending his shooting arm as high up as possible made his shot unblockable. There were even times when he released the ball when his hand was already above the rim.

This meant that Robertson had a big target in the paint. He could just simply dump the ball to Kareem in the middle and allow the big man to work. This was the first time The Big O had played with anyone standing over seven feet. Wayne Embry, the starting center that Robertson had during his prime years in Cincinnati, stood only 6'8". And this was also the first time that The Big O was going to play with someone who was arguably a better player than he was even at his prime.

On top of the fact that Oscar Robertson was about to enter his most successful season as a pro, he also was successful as a leader for the NBA players. As the president of the NBA Players Association, he was instrumental in filing a lawsuit against the NBA to suspend the proposed NBA-ABA merger until the league could solve its issues with free agency and player-locking.[i]

The merger initially looked good because it allowed more talents and more teams to enter the NBA. However, the problem was that the players no longer had a fallback option in case they were locked into a situation they did not like. Robertson was in the same boat several times in Cincinnati because the Royals management did not seem to value his contributions to the franchise. Had there been free agency back then, Robertson could have easily listened to offers from other teams when the Royals were trying to low-ball him with a bad offer.

In that regard, since the ABA was an option for players who wanted to leave their teams in the NBA, Robertson and the NBPA wanted to stop the merger from happening because players would be forced to stay with their own teams, regardless of whether or not they liked the situation. The only way for the NBA and the ABA to finally merge was for the NBA to solve matters regarding free agency and player-locking, and the merger was suspended until 1976. This is why Oscar Robertson's contributions to the NBA are more than just what he did on the court. Had he not fought the NBA's stringent rules regarding player-locking, it would have taken a long time for the league to finally decide to allow their players to choose where they wanted to play.

Going back to the court, Robertson and Abdul-Jabbar were supposed to become the biggest one-two punch combo in the league. However, there were doubts regarding whether or not they could coexist in one team. Or even if they did coexist, the others might end up resenting them because they were already accounting for more than half a million in player salaries per season. Robertson was making $280,000 per year while Abdul-Jabbar had a $1.4-million contract spread over five years. To that end, Wes Pavalon, who owned the team back then, said that the only way for Oscar to understand how good Kareem was and the only way for Kareem to know that Oscar was that good of a player was for them to start playing together.[i] The general manager scoffed at the idea that Robertson needed to always have the ball in his hands because no one else in Cincinnati was ever good enough to take the ball away from him.

Both the owner and the general manager trusted Robertson's abilities to a point where they were even willing to pay him his asking price before he was traded to Milwaukee. This was something that he never experienced back in Cincinnati, where the ownership, the front office, and his final coach as a Royal did not see his value as a player. It was indeed a great change of scenery for arguably the greatest all-around player in league history at that time. He had a front office that respected him and a center that knew when to deliver.

Robertson and Abdul-Jabbar were not close at first because they did not spend a lot of time off the court. However, when they eventually got to know more about one another, what Oscar realized was that Kareem was like him in the sense that they are both players that treat basketball as a business.

They were both no-nonsense people that did not like doing things that allowed them to get exposed to the media.

In today's NBA, the biggest superstars can be found everywhere. They are in commercials, on print and digital ads, and even in movies. On top of that, NBA superstars today love the limelight and are always in places where they can be seen. They like being in the spotlight of attention, and only a few players act in a more reserved manner that allows them to avoid too much attention. It might be true that Kareem could be seen in movies and ads, but he was someone who kept things private and was just as less likely to be seen in public. As a *Sports Illustrated* piece once said, "Oscar and Kareem did not like wasting any motion or energy on things that are not basketball-related".[i] They loved being efficient both on and off the court, and that was the biggest thing they had in common between them. Having that kind of an attitude from the team's best players allowed the other guys on the Bucks to absorb the same mentality.

When the season began, the Bucks were able to recover from a slow start and eventually became the league's most dangerous team. Robertson provided the outside abilities that the team did not have a year ago. He was the threat that prevented teams from ganging up on Kareem in the paint. On top of that, the former Lew Alcindor commanded enough attention in the paint that defenders played Robertson one-on-one instead of ganging up on him. This was probably the first time in his career since his college days that he was not the focus of defensive attention. And it was also the first time in more than a decade that he did not need to score 20 to 30 points for his team to win.

Then came his homecoming to Cincinnati on November 8, 1970. When his name was announced, nearly 10,000 people in the building cheered for him. Nobody wanted to watch the Royals that time because they were a bad team, but over double the average attendance of a Royals game came to cheer on Oscar in his homecoming. This was the very first time since 1956 that he was not playing for the people of Cincinnati, but they cheered him on anyway because he was the sole reason why they even watched the Royals.

As the season went on, the Bucks realized that they had a target on their back because the other teams were beginning to realize how dangerous they were with their center-point guard tandem. That was when Robertson started to become more of a leader to his younger teammates, who often became frustrated and made mistakes whenever they were roughed up by opposing defenses. And no one on the team complained about The Big O telling them to straighten up.

At one point, Jon McGlocklin told reporters that he respected the way Robertson shaped them up whenever they made mistakes. Kareem quickly seconded the motion to make sure that no reporter would ever think about trying to make a story about him and Oscar not seeing eye to eye.[i] Everyone on the team respected The Big O because, at that point in his career, he was a living legend that had been around the league for more than ten years and had achieved personal accolades that only Abdul-Jabbar could potentially achieve as well.

Speaking of Kareem, at one point in the season, he told reporters how fiery Robertson could get in timeouts because he was never too shy of telling his teammates to step up and to play better. The big man was thankful that he had Oscar on his team because he was not someone who could do that himself due to his reserved personality. But Robertson, although reserved as well, did not care about being a silent leader anymore because he wanted the championship that season. Abdul-Jabbar saw that his point guard was on a mission that year and that he wanted the championship right then and there.[i]

Oscar Robertson's leadership translated to one of the most dominant and most efficient seasons a team could ever have. The Milwaukee Bucks dominated their way to 66 wins, which were two wins shy of tying with the 68-win season that the Philadelphia 76ers had in 1967. On top of that, the Bucks became the first team in league history to average more than 50% from the field in a single season because of the fact that they were efficient with their shot selection.

Kareem Abdul-Jabbar won the MVP that season and went on to lead the league in scoring by averaging more than 31 points while shooting more than 57% from the floor. At that point in history, that was the most lopsided MVP win. Meanwhile, Robertson was no longer the one-man wrecking crew he used to be because he did not need to score 20 or more points to lead his team to a win. He averaged 19.4 points, 5.7 rebounds, and 8.2 assists for the Milwaukee Bucks.

At 32 years of age, Robertson no longer cared about the stats because he already had enough stats to last an entire lifetime. What he cared more about was to make sure that his teammates were contributing and were getting enough shot attempts that allowed them to score efficiently while alleviating the pressure off of their towering center. Still, he ended up with impressive numbers that 22-year old players in the league can only hope to have.

Thanks to the momentum they gained throughout the entire season, the Milwaukee Bucks had one of the most impressive postseason runs in league history. In the first round, they defeated the San Francisco Warriors, who had Nate Thurmond and Jerry Lucas manning the paint, in only five games. The victory was not only because of Kareem's dominance was also due to the fact that Robertson and Dandridge both contributed with timely baskets.

The second-round meeting against the Lakers was supposed to be one for the ages because that was when Wilt and Kareem met in the playoffs for the first time in NBA history. However, the deciding factor was Jerry West, who could not play a single playoff game due to a knee injury. As such, despite Wilt defending Kareem as well as any center could, the Bucks came away with a win in only five games as Oscar Robertson was on his way to the Finals for the first time in his career.

Surprisingly, the 42-win Baltimore Bullets defeated the New York Knicks in a seven-game series to reach the Finals. No one on that Bucks team wanted Baltimore to win because they were all gunning for New York, who had beaten them a year ago. And most of their plays and their programs had been tailored for the Knicks.

But that did not mean that they disrespected the Bullets, who had Wes Unseld, an undersized center but a former MVP and the only other player aside from Wilt to win the award in his rookie season. Nevertheless, the problem was that the Bullets did not have what it took to beat the Bucks. Earl Monroe was injured in the Knicks series. Wes Unseld was also suffering from a leg injury. And Gus Johnson had bad knees. So, when the NBA Finals came, Baltimore simply had no chance. Kareem was towering over both Unseld and Johnson, who were 6'7" and 6'6" respectively, in the paint. Meanwhile, no one on that Bullets backcourt could match up with Oscar Robertson, who went on to play the series of his life because he knew that he might not have another chance at a title.

In the end, the Bucks defeated the Bullets soundly in that series. Three of their four wins in that sweep were double-digit victories. Meanwhile, both Robertson and Abdul-Jabbar dominated their matchups. Oscar went on to average 23.5 points and 9.5 assists in that series. Meanwhile, Kareem played with the undersized Bullets frontline and averaged 27 points and 18.5 rebounds while shooting over 60% from the field.

The Bucks brewed the perfect storm in that Finals win as Robertson went on to win his first and only NBA championship after spending 11 long years in the NBA. All of those losing seasons and struggles with the front office in Cincinnati led to the one accomplishment that had eluded him for more than ten years. He was now a winner in every sense of the word.

After the Bucks won, Bullets head coach Gene Shue believed that Robertson should have won the Finals MVP because he was the man who controlled the pace for Milwaukee while also playing terrific defense. The MVP trophy went to Kareem, whom Oscar was happy for because he was completely dominant in that series. Robertson was simply happy that he won a championship.

In hindsight, had it not been for Robertson's timely intervention in 1970 and his lawyer, Jake Brown, he could have easily been a member of the Bullets. He might have even reached the Finals with Baltimore only to lose to the Bucks. He was glad that he had that he a veto clause in his contract and that he chose the right team to get traded to. Because he had that choice—the only time he ever had a choice ever since he was drafted by the Cincinnati Royals—he was able to become the winner that a lot of people doubted he could ever be in the NBA. The load on his shoulders was now lighter than ever.

The Final Years

When great players are being discussed, the one thing that people often talk about is their championships. Even today, a championship is what validates a person's greatness in the NBA, and that is why all of the great players continue to chase championship after championship. But there has been an overemphasis on the narrative that "championship" equals "greatness." People tend to put too much emphasis on a player's championship or lack thereof as they are quick to dismiss a player's greatness when he or she does not have a title. Truth be told, a lot of the all-time greats never won titles. Karl Malone, who retired second only to Kareem Abdul-Jabbar in career points scored, always came second and never won a title. Charles Barkley, arguably the second-biggest star of the early 90s, did not win one as well. And Steve Nash, a two-time MVP, did not win a title in his career.

In that regard, throughout Robertson's career, there was no arguing against the fact that he was great. One could say that he was the greatest point guard in NBA history from the 1960s up to the 70s. He was right up there together with Jerry West, who was more of a scoring point guard than a playmaker. With all due respect to the greatness of Bob Cousy, he had a better team around him and never had the stats that the likes of Robertson and West had.

But the one thing that people doubted about Oscar Robertson was his ability to win. He might have still ended his career as the greatest point guard in league history, with or without a title. Still, winning a championship was the validation he needed. It was the ultimate exclamation point that he needed to have to prove his status as an all-time great talent. And that was what the 1971 NBA championship meant to him, even though he was already way past his prime when he won that title and even though Kareem Abdul-Jabbar was no doubt the best player on that Bucks team.

Winning a championship allowed him to validate his greatness. He had already proven himself a great individual player with all the stats and the individual accolades he won throughout his entire career. But that championship was the cherry on top of what is still regarded as one of the greatest all-around careers the league has ever seen.

Like any champion, Robertson believed that he was not yet done chasing more championships. He was turning 33 during the 1971-72 season. In today's NBA, 33 can still be a player's prime years. But the equivalent of 33 in the 70s was the equivalent of 40 in today's modern era. All of the mileage and the wear and tear of physical basketball had already done their damage to Robertson's body. Still, he relented and was still playing exceptionally because the chance for a second straight championship was still in the books.

Then again, repeating as champions is easier said than done. Even though the Boston Celtics made it look easy back in the 60s when the league was not yet that competitive and when there were only fewer than ten teams in the NBA, it was still a major accomplishment for them to win all of those consecutive championships. However, not every team could be the Celtics, as all of the champions after Boston learned that the hard way.

Since the Celtics repeated as champions in 1969, the next team that did the same was in 1988. It took nearly two decades for another team to win two championships in consecutive years because the league was getting more and more competitive with all the new teams and the fresh new faces coming in to shake things up in the NBA. And that meant that repeating was also going to be tough for the Milwaukee Bucks.

The pressure for Larry Costello to do what Red Auerbach and Bill Russell did as head coaches probably got to him. Even though everyone on the team knew that they had a target on their backs, Costello only made life more difficult for them by drilling them harder. Robertson was already 33 during the 1971-72 season, and he no longer had the legs for college freshman drills.[i]

Still, the dream of a second championship was alive for Robertson. He might have been one of the older superstars in the league, along with Wilt Chamberlain and Jerry West. But he was still better than all of the other point guards in the NBA. This allowed him to put up 17.4 points and 7.7 assists in his second season with the Bucks.

It was ultimately a back issue that kept Robertson from staying at the top of his game. He suffered from sciatica, which kept him out of 18 games during the regular season. The Bucks still managed to win 63 games that year, but The Big O was not at his best during the playoffs. His back problems kept him from sprinting at full speed because there were times when he could not even feel his left leg. But that did not stop Milwaukee from dominating the Golden State Warriors in the first round. Robertson finished with 18 points, 6.4 rebounds, and 9.8 assists in the five games he played against the Warriors in the first round. Nevertheless, they had a big problem in the second round when they went up against the Los Angeles Lakers.

That season, the Lakers won a record of 33 straight games in a single regular season, a feat that still stands today. Despite banking on the aging legs of Wilt and Jerry, they still went on to win 69 wins in a single season, and that was a new record at that time. Today, only the 1995-96 Chicago Bulls (72 wins) and the 2015-16 Golden State Warriors (73 wins) have had more wins than that amazing Laker team under new head coach Bill Sharman.

The tables were turned on the Bucks in that series against the Lakers. That prior season, Milwaukee was the record-setting team and was almost completely healthy, while the Lakers did not even have Jerry West. In 1972, the Bucks' star point guard was hobbling while Los Angeles had the better record and a healthier team.

While Milwaukee won the first game in L.A. by 21 points, they could not match the depth and firepower of the Lakers, whose league-leading center and two-time MVP was nearly neutralized by Wilt Chamberlain. Meanwhile, Robertson only played seven minutes in Game 6 because of his injury. The Bucks only lost by four points in that final game, as they could have stretched the series to seven games had Oscar been healthy. As such, the dream of a consecutive title had been shattered right then and there by the Lakers.

Jerry West won his solitary NBA championship that year. He had been in the same boat as The Big O in the sense that he was an all-time great that could not validate his greatness with a championship. But he did so that season just a year after Robertson won his only title. After the 1972 season, arguably the four greatest players in NBA history at that time (Russell, Chamberlain, Robertson, and West) were already champions.

During the 1972-73 season, the Bucks once again had a chance to become great. They won 60 games during the regular season. But age had caught up with Robertson because he was going through the season with all sorts of different aches and pains. Averaging 15.5 points and 7.5 assists in the regular season, The Big O was not named an All-Star for the first time since he started his career in 1960. But he had already accomplished everything he could as an All-Star and was now looking to add more championships to his trophy case.

Unfortunately for the Bucks, they could not solve a 47-win Golden State Warriors in the first round. Despite being bigger and taller, Kareem struggled against Nate Thurmond when going up for rebounds. The Warriors were hungrier for the ball despite the fact that Robertson had a resurgent moment against them. In the Bucks' Game 3 victory, he finished with 34 points.

However, even though he was able to turn back the hands of time in that series, his efforts were not enough. Robertson's Milwaukee Bucks lost to the Golden State Warriors in six games. He averaged 21.2 points and 7.5 assists in that six-game series against the Warriors. It looked like he would no longer have the opportunity to play for a championship again after the Bucks lost in the first round just two years shy of their first championship in 1971.

After the 1973 postseason, Oscar Robertson's original three-year deal with the Bucks was done. But he believed that he still had one more run in his legs, and that was when he told Wayne Embry, who began working with the Bucks' front office after retiring, that he wanted to re-sign. The catch was that he was only going to take a one-year deal because he had already decided that he was going to retire at the end of the 1973-74 season. He announced to the media that he was returning for a one-year deal worth $250,000. Robertson also told the media that he was not planning to become a coach in the hopes of preventing the media from creating a story regarding him possibly replacing Costello in 1974.

Robertson, in preparation for what was to become his final run, slimmed down his weight and stayed lean without sacrificing the bulk that he needed to bully opposing guards. Keeping his weight within a manageable level allowed him to stay healthy and durable throughout much of the entire season despite being 35 years old. The only other elder statesman playing well was Jerry West, who was unfortunately marred by injuries in what also became his final season in the NBA.

Still, Robertson missed 12 games that season because of his back issues. But that did not matter because, at that point, he was only gunning for one more run at the title. The important part was that he was healthy in time for the playoffs, as Milwaukee went on to win a league-high of 59 games during the regular season and was just as dominant as ever. Kareem Abdul-Jabbar went on to win his third MVP award in a span of only five seasons. Meanwhile, Robertson played 70 games and averaged 12.7 points and 6.4 assists, the lowest numbers he ever had in his career.

Unfortunately, the Bucks lost Lucius Allen to a torn ligament in his knee right before the playoffs. He was supposed to be the guard that would take over the ball-handling duties after Robertson's retirement. But that injury prevented him from having what could have been a stellar career because he was already steadily rising as a capable point guard that could score, run the break, and pass. Allen's injury meant that Robertson was going to have to take on a bigger role during the postseason.

Despite losing a capable secondary guard like Allen, the Bucks were still rolling in the playoffs. Against an old and tired Lakers team that no longer had Wilt Chamberlain to guard Kareem Abdul-Jabbar, Milwaukee went on to win the series in five games. Then, in the second round, Abdul-Jabbar and Dandridge averaged around 60 points in total to sweep the Chicago Bulls. Robertson averaged 17 points and 10 assists in that series and thoroughly outplayed former teammate Norman Van Lier, who was an All-Star that season.

For only the second time in his career, Oscar Robertson was back in the Finals. It was only fitting that he was going up against a new generation of the Boston Celtics. The last time he faced Boston in the playoffs was during his younger years when he was striking fear into the hearts of Bill Russell and Bob Cousy. This time, he could no longer do that, but he could still provide the leadership that his team needed.

That Finals series against the Celtics turned out to be a back-and-forth affair between two teams that each had two members of the 75th Anniversary Team. Greatness was on display during the series because, despite being in the middle of their 30s, both Robertson and John Havlicek were playing well beyond what their age showed. Meanwhile, Kareem Abdul-Jabbar and Dave Cowens, the two best centers in the NBA at that time, were going neck and neck despite the size difference between them.

The two teams traded wins as Boston headed into Game 6 with a 3-2 lead over Milwaukee. Boston could have won the series on their home floor by winning Game 6. However, the Bucks stormed back in the fourth quarter to tie the game and send it to overtime. Then the game went to another overtime, as neither team wanted to give an inch. It was a game-winning skyhook that allowed the Bucks to have one more hope of winning a title as Milwaukee took the game by a solitary point to send the series to a seventh and deciding game in Wisconsin. Robertson played his best game in that double-overtime win as he played all 58 minutes and contributed 18 points and 10 assists.

Robertson's final NBA game, win or lose, was on May 12, 1974. He was playing in Milwaukee, and there was no better way for him to end his career than to hoist a championship in front of the home crowd. But that never happened. And this was when losing Lucius Allen greatly affected the Bucks as Oscar Robertson had all but emptied his gas tank in the 58 minutes he played two days before.

In his final game, Robertson was 2 out of 13 from the field and could not find the bottom of the bucket. The Big O may have had 11 assists, but Kareem could not handle the scoring load all on his own. It steadily became apparent that Boston was the deeper team in this series when they took a hard-fought seven-game Finals series from the Milwaukee Bucks. When John Havlicek, another old-timer in the NBA, was named the 1974 Finals MVP, he told the media that this was the most meaningful of his seven NBA championships. He went on to win eight in his career. Oscar Robertson came up to his fellow legend and, along with congratulating him, told him that he deserved it. As for The Big O, he had played his final game in the NBA.

After the Finals, Milwaukee kept Oscar Robertson on their active roster. Wayne Embry told him that the Bucks wanted him back on their team. But there was a big problem—they did not want to offer him the same contract that had the no-cut and no-trade clause. The thing about that clause was that the NBA was going to expand soon by adding two teams. Every team in the NBA was supposed to lose two players to the expansion teams. However, a player that had a no-cut and no-trade clause was exempt from getting drafted by the expansion teams. Embry told Robertson that the Bucks president was not willing to offer him a contract that had that clause because they did not want to lose their younger players. NBA rules at that time required that, for Robertson to re-sign with the Bucks, he had to sign the same contract he had a year ago.[i]

By August of 1974, Robertson had yet to announce his retirement because the Bucks still kept his name on the active roster. However, when CBS called to tell him that they had an opening for him as a basketball analyst, he thought about accepting the job even though he had spent an eternity avoiding the media during his basketball career. Robertson told them that he was willing to listen to their offer.

On August 24, 1974, it was finally announced that Oscar Robertson was now retired from the game of basketball. After 14 seasons in the NBA, he finished with dazzling numbers. He was first all-time in assists and second all-time behind only Wilt Chamberlain in points scored. At that point, his status as one of the all-time greats was clear. But it was time for him to leave the game to the younger generations that were inspired by his greatness.

Today, there are still plenty of great NBA players that may not have been old enough to watch Oscar Robertson play but are very similar to him when it comes to his all-around greatness and tenacity on the hardwood floor. The torch may have been passed down from guys like LeBron, Scottie, and Magic. But the one who carried it first and passed it down was Oscar "The Big O" Robertson.

Chapter 5: Post-NBA

Right after retiring from the NBA, Oscar Robertson signed a deal with CBS to become a color commentator in the network's coverage of the NBA games. He was a rookie in that field as he needed to go through a crash course on sports broadcasting. Of course, he also worked with a voice coach that taught him how to lose his thick Tennessee accent.

Sadly, at that time, Robertson was a bit too slick with the way he commentated because he was open and honest about his thoughts when calling the game. When officiating was bad, he called it that way. And because there were still tensions regarding his lawsuit, he was eventually fired from his role as a commentator. During the 1974-75 seasons, however, the Kansas City Kings, which was the former Royals team, decided to retire Robertson's #14. The number is still retired up to this day, even after the Kings moved to Sacramento. Eventually, the Milwaukee Bucks decided to retire his #1 jersey as well in honor of arguably the best point guard the franchise has ever had, even if it was only for four short years.

Throughout his entire post-NBA life, Robertson stayed out of the spotlight because he was always a reserved man. He focused more on the business aspect of his life and decided to stay in Cincinnati, where he and his family lived for a very long time during his NBA years. However, in 2004, he did serve as interim head coach of the Cincinnati Bearcats for about a month. Then, in 2006, he, John Wooden, Bill Russell, Dean Smith, and Dr. James Naismith became the founding member of the National Collegiate Basketball Hall of Fame.[v]

Oscar Robertson spent most of his days out of the limelight, despite his status as one of the greatest players in NBA history. Then, in 2021, he was named one of the members of the NBA's 75th Anniversary Team. In February 2022, ESPN ranked Robertson ninth on their list of players that were included in the 75th Anniversary Team. Only Tim Duncan, Larry Bird, Bill Russell, Wilt Chamberlain, Magic Johnson, Kareem Abdul-Jabbar, LeBron James, and Michael Jordan are ahead of him on the ESPN ranking.[vi]

Chapter 6: Personal Life

Oscar Robertson was born in Tennessee to parents Mazell and Bailey Robertson. He has two brothers, Bailey Jr. and Henry, who both played basketball as well. Ever since 1960, he has been married to the same woman, Yvonne, who he met while he was still playing for the University of Cincinnati. He was an incoming sophomore when he was introduced to Yvonne, who was born to a middle-class family, thanks in large part to how her father was able to establish a tailoring business. As such, she never had to undergo the same kind of poverty that Oscar went through when he was a boy. She graduated from the University of Cincinnati just a few months before Robertson started going to the same school in 1956. Four years later, they were married shortly after Oscar graduated from college.

While Oscar was in college, Yvonne worked on her Master's degree. She was able to get a teaching job while Oscar was playing in the NBA. During the time when The Big O was dominating the professional league, Yvonne spent most of her days taking care of the kids. Oscar and Yvonne have three daughters, Mari, Shana Yvonne, and Tia, to whom Oscar gave one of his kidneys after she was diagnosed with kidney failure.

During his NBA years, Oscar Robertson was also the president of the NBA Players' Association, a union group started by Bob Cousy during the 50s. It was thanks to his leadership that the players were able to demand more from NBA teams, as there was a stark increase in salaries when Robertson was sitting as the president of the union.

After his years in the NBA, he has mostly kept out of the spotlight and is always with his family back in Cincinnati while attending to the different businesses he invested in with the money he earned as an NBA player.

Robertson enjoys woodworking during his spare time.[vii] But he still attends the home games of the University of Cincinnati, where he finished his college career as the greatest player the program has ever produced.

Chapter 7: Impact and Legacy

When people think about Oscar Robertson's impact on the game of basketball, the things that often come to mind are the triple-doubles he has put up during his entire NBA career. It is true that he was the man who revolutionized what it meant to be truly all-around because he had the size, athleticism, and skills that allowed him to dominate his position.

At 6'5" and more than 200 pounds, Robertson played at a time when all of the other point guards were 6'1" and shorter. He had the size of a prototypical forward but had the skills of a point guard. This allowed him to handle the ball all the time and dish out assists at an all-time pace during the height of his NBA career. And because the pace of the game was faster during his time, he was able to help out on the rebounding end and went on to average double digits in rebounds three times in his career.

Of course, thanks to the skill level he had at his size, he dominated as a scorer and went on to average 30 or more points regularly during his prime years in Cincinnati. He ended his career with a total of 26,710 points scored and was only second to Wilt Chamberlain in that category when he retired.

Altogether, Robertson had the package that allowed him to compile a career total of 181 triple-doubles, the most in the NBA for 47 years since he retired from the game. It was only on May 11, 2021, when Russell Westbrook broke Robertson's record for all-time triple-doubles collected.[viii] Westbrook was also the same person who was even with Robertson as the only other player to average a triple-double in a single season. Robertson did that in 1962, and it took 55 years until another player accomplished the same feat.

Given those numbers, it is completely understandable why Oscar Robertson is the progenitor of the elite all-around player archetype in the history of the NBA. Before his time, players were either great scorers, great rebounders, or both. Those who could set their teammates up were not entirely the best at scoring the ball. However, when Robertson entered the league, he became the first person who could basically do it all because he could score, rebound, and make plays, all at elite levels. Arguably the only other player who had the capacity to do that during the 1960s was Wilt Chamberlain, who led the league in total assists at one point in his career. But not even he could average the same all-around numbers that Robertson was putting up during a time when the best NBA players could easily pile up stats thanks to how the competitive level of the league was far from what it is today.

It was only during the time of Magic Johnson's dominance as an all-around player that people realized Robertson's prowess at scoring triple-doubles w was far greater than the Laker legend.[i] In fact, It was Magic Johnson who became the league's newest all-around threat more than half a decade after Oscar Robertson retired from the game. Since then, more and more all-around threats have entered the league. Players such as Scottie Pippen, Penny Hardaway, Grant Hill, Jason Kidd, LeBron James, Russell Westbrook, Nikola Jokić, and Luka Dončić have all become special players that could easily put up triple-doubles during their respective eras. And anyone can trace that all-around greatness back to Robertson, but only Westbrook was able to accomplish what he did when he averaged a triple-double.

The fact that it took 55 years for another player to average a triple-double in a single season speaks volumes about how special Robertson's greatness was during his prime years. After his days in the NBA, players became bigger, more skilled, and more athletic, but none of them aside from Westbrook were able to duplicate what The Big O had accomplished. And for more than five decades, no one thought that any player could accomplish that feat again because it was becoming even more difficult for players to sustain that level of excellence for an entire 82-game stretch.

Robertson's ability to sustain that elite level of excellence was what was truly great about the fact that he averaged a triple-double. With all due respect to Russell Westbrook, players during the 60s were playing under conditions that were a lot worse. Despite that, Robertson was still able to achieve something that only one other player had ever done before. And he once said that had he known that the triple-double average was going to be something that is celebrated today, he would have done it multiple times in his career.

Thanks to his all-around greatness, he inspired an entire generation of playmakers that did not only pass but also scored. Before Robertson's time, point guards were simply passers that brought the ball up the floor and dictated the tempo. Bob Cousy was a great scorer during his prime, but he was not at the level of Robertson when it came to his ability to take over a game with his scoring. In today's NBA, the standard for a point guard is for him to be able to both pass and score. There is no room for a pure playmaking point guard that cannot score in today's NBA because this position has become the most important role in the modern-day guard-oriented league. And Robertson could have certainly averaged 30 points, 10 rebounds, and 10 assists had he played today.

On top of him impacting the game to help turn it into what it is today, Robertson also left a lasting legacy in the Royals/Kings franchise. Since he left the Royals, the team struggled to become relevant again, as the franchise had to relocate several times before it finally settled in Sacramento as the

Kings we know today. But even after relocating to Sacramento, the Kings never had a player as great as Oscar Robertson. This is why The Big O still holds most of the major records in Sacramento. He is the team's all-time leading scorer by a wide margin. He also holds the record for the franchise's all-time assists, as he has more than twice the career assists of the man who is second on the list. Impressive enough, he is also third in career rebounds in the Royals' franchise despite playing the point guard spot. And no other player in franchise history has ever come close to his status as the greatest player the Royals/Kings franchise has ever seen.

While he did only spend four seasons with the Milwaukee Bucks, he still left a lasting legacy on that franchise because he was the first starting point guard that led the team to a title. It took fifty years for Jrue Holiday to help the team win another championship as the starting point guard for the Milwaukee Bucks, who won the championship in 2021. Because he ran the team's offense to perfection during his four years with the franchise, the Bucks were championship contenders until he retired. During the 1974-75 season, the first year without Robertson, the Bucks did not even make the playoffs.

It is tough not to think about all of the stats and the individual and team accomplishments when Oscar Robertson is the topic of the conversation. After all, he did put up stats that everyone thought were impossible to duplicate until someone else did it. However, what many people do not realize is the fact that Robertson's biggest impact on the game of basketball happened outside the regular confines of the hardwood floor. In his capacity as the president of the NBPA during the 60s and early 70s, Robertson instituted a suit that prevented the NBA from merging with the ABA in 1970 on antitrust grounds. While the merger looked good on paper, it was a problem for the players in the NBA.

When the ABA began in 1967, basketball players now had a backup in case they did not want to play in the NBA. The problem with the NBA back then was that a player could not sign with another team regardless of what his contract situation was with the team that drafted him. It was only the franchise that drafted the player that could renegotiate a player's contract. The only way for a player to move to a different franchise was via a trade. So, if a team did not want to trade a player, they could low-ball him into accepting a bad contract while playing for a team that he did not want to play for. The rise of the ABA gave players a chance to sign with a different team in a different league because doing so was not against the NBA's rules. However, because the NBA was about to merge with the ABA in 1970, what would have happened was that the players would no longer be able to choose to play in the ABA if they did not like the situation with their NBA team. Robertson was in that position numerous times in his career when the Cincinnati Royals tried to low-ball him into signing a contract that did not reflect his value to the franchise.

The Robertson lawsuit prevented the merger until the NBA could fix the issues that the players had regarding their status with their respective teams. They did not want the teams that drafted them to hold their rights indefinitely. But when the NBA players ran out of money to pay for the lawsuit against the league, a settlement was agreed upon in 1976. This settlement allowed the NBA-ABA merger to happen while also introducing free agency in incremental stages.[ix] It was only in 1988 that Tom Chambers became the very first unrestricted free agent in league history.[x] Since then, other sports leagues throughout America instituted their own free agency as well. Players are now free to choose where they want to play, all thanks to the fact that Oscar Robertson and the other NBA players in 1970 instituted a suit against the league itself. Had he not done that, it might have been another decade or so for the NBA to finally recognize free agency as a right that the players needed to have.

The Oscar Robertson Suit, as it is often called, paved the way for LeBron James' "The Decision" in 2010. It helped open up the floodgates for the massive $250 million contracts that the best NBA players have in today's league, as teams are now forced to pay their players insane amounts to keep their players from moving to other teams that are willing to give them what they are worth.

The player empowerment era started because one man decided that he and his fellow players needed to be empowered and needed to be free back in 1970. It happened to be a Black American that started the suit at a time when African-American citizens were not yet as free as they are today. Oscar Robertson's bravery to fight for what he believed in allowed the NBA to become one of the most valuable sports leagues in the entire world today. That is why Robertson's impact on the game of basketball and the NBA is more than just the stats that he earned and the awards that he won.

When players that dominated the 60s are talked about, it is often said that there will never be another [insert player name here]. It is the same case for Oscar Robertson, even though there are now other players that can put up stats that are just as impressive or even more impressive than what he had back in his prime. Nevertheless, he not only had ridiculous stats, but he also inspired an entire generation to play the way he did and to lead the way he did both on and off the court. That is the reason why it is not a stretch to say that there will never be another Oscar Robertson in the history of the NBA.

Final Word/About the Author

I was born and raised in Norwalk, Connecticut. Growing up, I could often be found spending many nights watching basketball, soccer, and football matches with my father in the family living room. I love sports and everything that sports can embody. I believe that sports are one of the most genuine forms of competition, heart, and determination. I write my works to learn more about influential athletes in the hopes that from my writing, you the reader can walk away inspired to put in an equal if not greater amount of hard work and perseverance to pursue your goals. If you enjoyed *Oscar Robertson: The Inspiring Story of One of Basketball's Greatest Point Guards*, please leave a review! Also, you can read more of my works on *David Ortiz, Mike Trout, Bryce Harper, Jackie Robinson, Aaron Judge, Odell Beckham Jr., Bill Belichick, Serena Williams, Rafael Nadal, Roger Federer, Novak Djokovic, Richard Sherman, Andrew Luck, Rob Gronkowski, Brett Favre, Calvin Johnson, Drew Brees, J.J. Watt, Colin Kaepernick, Aaron Rodgers, Peyton Manning, Tom Brady, Russell Wilson, Odell Beckham Jr., Bill Belichick, Charles Barkley, Trae Young, Gregg Popovich, Pat Riley, John Wooden, Steve Kerr, Brad Stevens, Red Auerbach, Doc Rivers, Erik Spoelstra, Michael Jordan, LeBron James, Kyrie Irving, Klay Thompson, Stephen Curry, Kevin Durant, Russell Westbrook, Anthony Davis, Chris Paul, Blake Griffin, Kobe Bryant, Joakim Noah, Scottie Pippen, Carmelo Anthony, Kevin Love, Grant Hill, Tracy McGrady, Vince Carter, Patrick Ewing, Karl Malone, Tony Parker, Allen Iverson, Hakeem Olajuwon, Reggie Miller, Michael Carter-Williams, John Wall, James Harden, Tim Duncan, Steve Nash, Draymond Green, Kawhi Leonard, Dwyane Wade, Ray Allen, Pau Gasol, Dirk Nowitzki, Jimmy Butler, Paul Pierce, Manu Ginobili, Pete Maravich, Larry Bird, Kyle Lowry, Jason Kidd, David Robinson, LaMarcus*

Aldridge, Derrick Rose, Paul George, Kevin Garnett, Chris Paul, Marc Gasol, Yao Ming, Al Horford, Amar'e Stoudemire, DeMar DeRozan, Isaiah Thomas, Kemba Walker, Chris Bosh, Andre Drummond, JJ Redick, DeMarcus Cousins, Wilt Chamberlain, Bradley Beal, Rudy Gobert, Aaron Gordon, Kristaps Porzingis, Nikola Vucevic, Andre Iguodala, Devin Booker, John Stockton, Jeremy Lin, Chris Paul, Pascal Siakam, Jayson Tatum, Gordon Hayward, Nikola Jokic, Bill Russell, Victor Oladipo, Luka Doncic, Ben Simmons, Shaquille O'Neal, Joel Embiid, Donovan Mitchell, Damian Lillard and *Giannis Antetokounmpo* in the Kindle Store. If you love basketball, check out my website at claytongeoffreys.com to join my exclusive list where I let you know about my latest books and give you lots of goodies.

Like what you read? Please leave a review!

I write because I love sharing the stories of influential athletes like Oscar Robertson with fantastic readers like you. My readers inspire me to write more so please do not hesitate to let me know what you thought by leaving a review! If you love books on life, basketball, or productivity, check out my website at claytongeoffreys.com to join my exclusive list where I let you know about my latest books. Aside from being the first to hear about my latest releases, you can also download a free copy of *33 Life Lessons: Success Principles, Career Advice & Habits of Successful People*. See you there!

Clayton

References

[i] Robertson, O. (2013). *The Big O: My Life, My Times, My Game*. Bison Books.

[ii] "Oscar Robertson". *NBA.com*. Web.

[iii] "Oscar Robertson". *Encyclopedia.com*. Web.

[iv] Kurkijan, Tim. "Willie Mays at 90 -- He was Steph Curry, Michael Jordan, Simone Biles and Mikhail Baryshnikov". *ESPN*. 6 May 2021. Web.

[v] "Wooden, Russell lead founding class into Collegiate Hall of Fame". *NABC.com*. 20 November 2006. Web.

[vi] "The NBA's 75th Anniversary Team, ranked: Where 76 basketball legends check in on our list". *ESPN*. 21 February 2022. Web.

[vii] *TheBigO.com*. Web.

[viii] "Russell Westbrook breaks Oscar Robertson's triple-double record". *NBA.com*. 11 May 2021. Web.

[ix] Smith, Sam. "How Oscar Robertson's Lawsuit Vs. NBA Paved Way To Today's Massive Contracts". *The Post Game*. 21 November 2017. Web.

[x] "Tom Chambers: The First Unrestricted Free Agent". *NBA.com*. 2 June 2014. Web.

Printed in Great Britain
by Amazon